Reflections on
My Call to Preach

For
Nettie Lee

Reflections on My Call to Preach

Connecting the Dots

FRED BRENNING CRADDOCK

CHALICE
PRESS
ST. LOUIS, MISSOURI

Scripture quotations marked NRSV are from the *New Revised Standard Version Bible,* copyright 1989, Division of Christian Education of the National Council of the Churches of Christ in the United States of America. Used by permission. All rights reserved.

Cover image: GettyImages
Cover and interior design: Elizabeth Wright

Visit Chalice Press on the World Wide Web at
www.chalicepress.com

10 9 8 7 6 5 4 3 2 1   09 10 11 12 13

Library of Congress Cataloging-in-Publication Data

Craddock, Fred B.

Reflections on my call to preach : connecting the dots / Fred Brenning Craddock.

p. cm.

ISBN 978-0-8272-3257-0

1. Vocation—Christianity. 2. Preaching. 3. Craddock, Fred B. I. Title.

BV4740.C73 2009
286.6092--dc22
[B]

2009008692

Printed in United States of America

Contents

Preface   vii

Introduction   1

1. Before I Was Born   5

2. If You Will Let Him Live   13

3. The Midwife   21

4. My Mother   29

5. My Father   39

6. Three to a Bed   49

7. School Days   57

8. School Days (Continued)   65

9. Sunday School   73

10. Staying for Church   83

11. Bethany Hills   93

12. The Summer of '46   103

13. Reflections on These Reflections   113

Preface

When first I was asked by Chalice Press to write a small volume on The Call to Preach, I was comfortable with saying "Yes"; the subject was as familiar as my own life, and the twelve months to prepare the manuscript was enough and to spare. Then a problem arose; the subject was as unfamiliar as my own life. At the end of twelve months, I had not one sentence. Difficulties bred difficulties.

When personal memory is one's primary resource, one has to accept that remembering is not repeating. More than retrieval of deposited events is involved. When a boy's tomorrow is related as yesterday, the firmest commitment to honest reporting must not claim disinterested accuracy. Even in a pledge to the truth and nothing but the truth, reader and writer acknowledge that memory leaks and twists.

The temptation to silence is almost overwhelming. For example, the material is very personal; who will read it, and where, and why? Once the words are released, all ownership is relinquished. Private words become public words at a price: the loss of intention. Added to the temptation to protect oneself is the felt need to satisfy the reader with recollections that are readily portable to the reader's life and experiences. "Very helpful" is a response devoutly to be wished, but honesty resists tugs toward rewriting one's life. And very early in the writing it becomes inescapably clear that this is not about me alone. I was, and am, a member of a family. I had parents and siblings. I had friends, and schoolmates, and teachers. And there was the church with its fellowship, its teachers, and its ministers. Memories of them are vital to the story, but who wants to inflict pain even when adhering to the worthy purpose of "telling it like it was"?

Perhaps the strongest temptation is to write of certainty when there was no certainty. A vision, a voice, an extraordinary constellation of events to silence doubters and those who constantly repeat "what a coincidence": that would be helpful. Who wants to tell a story that is little more than a modest witness to the modesty of God?

In these pages I have attempted to be honest about my early life and respectful of those whose lives touched mine. If this recital prompts a reader to lay aside the book and to lay a new claim on his or her own history, risking an encounter with God in the process, then I will have been amply rewarded. In that hope, I trust you with these words.

My gratitude to Cyrus White, President and Publisher of the Christian Board of Publication, who patiently encouraged me past my hesitations, and to Pablo Jiménez, the Chalice Press editor who first contacted me about the project and would not leave me alone, calling into being what did not exist. And my thanks to Tammy Blair, more than a secretary, who converted my handwritten copy into a manuscript acceptable to the editor. Any errors in the book are as much mine as the rest of it, and I share ownership of them with no one.

Fred Brenning Craddock
Cherry Log, Georgia
September, 2008

Introduction

There are three times when one can know an event: in advance of it, as in rehearsal, or as in a classroom in preparation; at the time of the event, while it is going on, as in a wedding, or as in a baptism, or as in a military skirmish; or following the event, when it is over, in reflection on it, as after a sermon, or after a debate, or after a trip. Each perspective has limitations, but the one offering the most understanding is reflection or memory. Memory suffers from unwarranted criticism. Of course, we have all known since Psychology 101 that memory leaks and twists and even erases the unpleasant. We know that remembering is more than a simple transaction of deposit and retrieval. Memory is more like a flowing river, being affected by the land through which it moves. And once we accept that remembering is more than, and different from, repeating, then we are ready to embrace memory as a primary source of understanding, of identity, of hope.

I say this to alert the reader to the fact that the following pages are memory sketches, notations on recollections, and as such bear the traits of all remembering. The perception is offered as the reality, without historical documents to confirm or to contradict what is narrated. In preparation for writing, no research was done; with the majority of these episodes there was none to be done. Of course, I could have gone to a library or a courthouse to get the proper spelling of a name, to confirm the accuracy of a date, or to be sure of the number of children in a household. But I didn't; these certainties would add nothing to the story. Besides, historical research is difficult to restrain. Once begun, it grows, consuming time and offering attractive detours. Before long one is into genealogies, which take us to Adam and Eve and the question, what was I doing that brought me here? It seemed wise not to go down that road.

I did at the outset have a conversation with the oldest living member of my family, a cousin in her mid-nineties, in order to get confirmation of a certain name. The conversation failed; she suffers from dementia. I should also acknowledge two other "research" efforts. Within a year of this writing I enjoyed a brief reunion with my two surviving siblings, Al and Roland. We were at Al's home, which is not many miles from our birthplace. The location itself prompted remembering. At one point I tried to steer the conversation in the direction of our father. The trip stalled out rather quickly and so we moved in another direction. The third attempt to undergird my memories with verifiable information was going with the two of them to the three places we had lived in the growing-up years. Of the two houses in town in which we had lived, one remains, but, were it not for the address, we would not have known it was once our home. The trip to the farm where we were born was depressing. The house is gone, all the out buildings are gone, the land is not cultivated, and instead of cotton, corn, and tomatoes are briars, weeds, and underbrush. My research ended. Photographs of grandparents, parents, and siblings exist, of course, but none of them informed my search. The reader will have to be content with my memories; there will be no footnotes. But no matter: nothing here is offered as normative, nor enviable—maybe not even portable. I certainly hope there is nowhere in these pages any implied claim that an experience of mine, or the sum total of them, constitutes the way one is called of God. No one's experience circumscribes truth; much that is true and of God occurs while I am asleep, totally unaware.

These efforts at recall focus on the first eighteen years of my life; that is, up until I arrived at college in preparation for Christian ministry. I chose to confine myself to these years because they were formative. Just how formative the early years are was recently confirmed to me on a visit to Toronto. I was there to preach and the host church quartered me elegantly. I enjoyed the hospitality of a hotel for retirees, retirees who could afford the luxury of the place. Every guest had every need anticipated and cared for, in style. Dinner was formal—in dress, in tableware, in food, in service. During these splendid meals, luxurious and abundant, I noticed many guests took from their tables small packets of sweetener, salt, pepper, and cream. They stealthily put these in pockets and purses. I was stunned. On the day of my departure, I called my observation to the attention of the manager. I didn't want to be a snitch; I wanted an interpretation. He smiled, said he knew, and every two weeks, when guests were at dinner, workers went into the rooms and cleared out the contraband. "You see," he said, "all the guests here, in their early years, experienced the Great Depression." Obviously, all the later years of prosperity did not fully erase the uncertainty, the economic privation, and the fear of hunger. I have enjoyed sixty years of full and fulfilling ministry but, no doubt, the early years have left their footprints on me. If I could call up those years, I told myself, perhaps I could locate persons, places, and events that God used to direct my life toward ministry.

But it has not been easy, in part because of my chronological distance from those years. One can add to that hurdle that many powerful experiences of persons, places, and events come between today and my childhood and youth. Such memories tend to dwarf earlier ones. Old black-and-white flickering film is no match for High Definition and color. And I am sure some person or place or event of the earlier years now lies hidden behind larger, more vivid episodes, beyond memory's ability to retrieve.

Of course, not every memory can be entertained and included in this narrative. Not all qualify, but having said that raises the question of how *any* memory qualifies. If I hold "Called to Preach" as a magnet over my early years, then I would find what I was looking for. Some of such circular thinking is probably unavoidable, but I think I can honestly say I am open to discoveries, positive and negative, clear and vague, persuasive and contradictory, and therefore able to maintain respect for God's speaking and God's silence. I certainly do not want to bend the stories of my life to make them fit a desired pattern and move my life to an inevitable end. I have called this exercise "Connecting the Dots," but the reader should know that I do not know where all the dots are. To this day, "God called" and "I decided" are experienced as two sides of the same coin. I did not know in my first eighteen years, but since have learned the truth of Paul's unusual word to a church: "work out your own salvation with fear and trembling; for it is God who is at work in you, enabling you both to will and to work for his good pleasure" (Phil. 2:12b–13, NRSV).

The pages that follow, therefore, record my memories as I sit on my own shoulder, but I do not at any time sit on God's shoulder. To do so would be to view life's fabric from the pattern side. To use a common analogy, the underside of embroidery is a tangle of threads with no discernible design; the upper side bears the pattern: clear, intentional, and meaningful. One lives one's whole life viewing the underside, but trusting there is design not yet in sight. For some, faith is so strong that those believers claim glimpses of the design. Only a person who sits on God's shoulder has such a perspective. As you will notice from these pages, I do not sit there. But you will also notice that I believe God is active in the shaping of my life. Of that I have no doubt.

1

Before I Was Born

"My name is Brenning Craddock." So I responded to the woman helping to herd college freshmen through orientation. "Your name?" she asked, not even looking up, her voice quite indifferent. "Brenning Craddock," I repeated. "Beg pardon?" "Brenning Craddock." "I'm sorry?" "Brenning Craddock" "You'll have to spell it." "F-R-E-D." She felt my disgust and said, "Next; your name please." Thus began the life of Fred Craddock.

Actually, I was already Fred; Fred Brenning, as was my father. Although bearing the same name, our identities were different in the family and in the community: he was Fred; I was Brenning. My three brothers and I all used our middle names; William Walter was Walter, John Alvin was Alvin, Louis Roland was Roland, Fred Brenning was Brenning. Granted, sometimes my name was a problem. "Brennen" some said; "Brennan" some wrote. A close friend named his firstborn "Brennan," after me, he said. Even my daughter named my first grandson after me. "Brennan," said the birth announcement. "But, Laura, that's not my name." "I know, but that's the way everyone says it and spells it." Oh, well, it was sometimes a burden to me, too. "Be sure you write your full name on your paper before you turn it in." I did, but again I was the last one out to the playground.

As a child, more than once I quizzed my father about our common name. My questions were two. One, why was I, the fourth child and third son, named after him? Why not Walter, my oldest brother? After one of his usual cock-and-bull stories (I think it involved a revelation from a passing hobo), he said the midwife assured him that the first child would be a boy, as was obvious by the unborn "riding high" in the womb. The boy would be named Fred Brenning Jr. When Momma brought forth her first born she was not named Fred but Frieda. Daddy said he and Momma dropped the plan for a Junior, returning to it when it was my turn to be born.

Question two: In a family that named children after relations, why was he Fred Brenning? I never heard of a cousin Fred or grandpa Fred or uncle Fred. As for Brenning, I never heard of anybody anywhere in the world named that. It seemed weird. I braced myself for a story, and I got one. This one seemed true, but he was such a masterful storyteller, all his tales seemed true. Usually I didn't care whether his stories were true or false; they did their work, creating alternative worlds in which I could live. But I had something at stake in this one; this was my name we were talking about. For some reason it seemed important to me: was there somewhere at sometime a person who was the source of my name? If so, who was he? What did he do? What kind of person was he? Did I carry in my mind, my body, and my blood something more of this person than his name? I needed to know. I couldn't ask Grandmother Craddock; she was dead. Nor Grandfather Craddock; he, too, was dead. I asked Momma. She was a latecomer to the Craddock clan, knowing none of them until she met my father, but did she know if what he told me was true? I could believe her. She had an uncanny ability to distinguish between fact and fiction. I had many times been impaled on her sword of truth: "Did you go swimming in Sugar Creek? Did you lose your report card?

Is this all the change Mr. Cook gave you?" She and the truth were inseparable.

"Is what Daddy told me about his name and mine the truth?"

"Yes."

"But how do you know it is not one of his stories?"

"His mother told me. She named him. She ought to know."

I was satisfied. Almost.

Before I tell you the story, I need to explain the "almost." You see, Grandma Craddock's maiden name was Collinsworth. I realize that is a fact without significance to most of you, but it is of immense significance to every Craddock who came from Wales to settle in Virginia, North Carolina, Tennessee, and Texas. The Collinsworths and the Craddocks, neighbors in rural Crockett and Gibson Counties of West Tennessee, prospered as landowners and farmers, intermarried, and continued to prosper. Then the feud of the early twentieth century tarnished both families. No need to explore here the causes; it is enough to say two deaths were ruled accidental, one self-defense, and one shrouded in mystery. A gunfight in the Territory of New Mexico took the life of a Collinsworth. Court records there closed the books on the case: an escalating dispute between neighbors, a "fair" fight; no one was charged. No Craddock was mentioned.

Deaths ended but animosity and colorful stories did not. Thirty years after the feud I took a train to Columbia, Missouri, to visit my brother Walter, a journalism student at the university there. On the return trip, the elderly conductor refused to accept my ticket. "Why? No question was raised when I purchased the ticket." "We don't stop in Humboldt," said the conductor. "Why not?" "Too dangerous" he said. "I don't understand." "If the Craddocks don't kill you, the Collinsworths will." I took out my wallet, showed my identity, he sat down, explained that he was making a joke. Early in his career on the railroad, he always got the latest news about the feud when the train stopped in Humboldt. "No offense intended." "None taken."

The feud, the stories, even the memories are gone. I once attended a party with a Collinsworth girl. My wife is related by marriage to the Collinsworths. Hostilities, even suspicions, have ceased. But in the early 1930s, raising a question about what a Collinsworth told a Craddock, and vice versa, was not surprising. But my mother was certain: what Grandma Craddock (nee Collinsworth) told her about the origin of the name Fred Brenning was the truth. Here is what Momma said Grandma said.

Daddy was born in the evening of December 5, 1888, and his name was waiting for him. It had been since his conception. Grandma was a faithful member of the Methodist Episcopal Church, South. She was especially serious about John Wesley's accent on sanctification, which translated into strict moral and ethical instruction in the home as well as the church. As the mother of one daughter and several sons, Grandma was determined to bring them up in the "nurture and admonition of the Lord." Whatever else such nurture and admonition involved, it certainly included no alcohol, no tobacco, no card playing, no dancing, no profanity, no lying or stealing, and, of course, strict observance of the Sabbath. Even this partial list of "Thou shalts" and "Thou shalt nots" makes it clear Grandma would need wisdom, encouragement, and, to put it bluntly, backup. A friend at church suggested a book she had recently read which would re-enforce the Bible, inform, and perhaps inspire her sons, including the newborn in her arms. The book was written for boys, and was about a special boy. That special boy was named Fred Brenning.

Grandma acquired the book, read it with appetite and approval, and tried (successfully? unsuccessfully?) to get her older sons to read it. So impressed was Grandma that she told Grandpa that when their next child was born, and if it was a boy, he would be named Fred Brenning. Grandpa offered no objection although he very likely never read the book. All that

Momma related to me about the book was that it was a biography of a boy who was rescued from wild and unruly companions by a Sunday school teacher, concerned relatives, and several itinerant preachers of the Methodist Episcopal Church, South. The boy eventually heard and responded to the call to preach, a call to which he was faithful, overcoming many obstacles and hardships along the way. He became widely known, in and out of the church, and much admired. Based on my mother's report, it is no wonder Grandma became enthralled with Fred Brenning and wanted to pass his name and, hopefully, I am sure, his many Christian virtues, to her son.

I do not know if Grandma entertained a prayerful hope that her son would grow up to be a preacher like the first Fred Brenning. She may have, but if she did, she never voiced that hope to her son. At least, that is what my father said. On one occasion, when I was a pre-teen, I raised the subject with him.

"Did Grandma want you to be a preacher like the man after whom you were named?"

"I never was a member of the Methodist Church."

"I know that, but did she want you to be a preacher of any kind?"

"If she did, she never said so to me."

"Did you ever think about being a preacher?"

"I never gave the notion a moment's thought. Why do you ask?"

"I don't know; I was just wondering."

I do not recall ever again raising the subject. I did learn later of a series of wounds inflicted by the church on Daddy's family that seemed more painful to him than to the other family members. In due season, as an adolescent my father joined a church (The Christian Church [Disciples of Christ]) but remembered pains made his membership something less than one of full commitment. I will talk more of this matter at a later time when I explore my relation to my father. But not now.

I was satisfied by the story of the source of the name Fred Brenning and I put the story to bed. As a child I was proud to be named for my father who was named for a preacher. As a youth, I was silent about it, even on one occasion denying the "rumor" in a circle of friends who were ready to lay on me nicknames that would convey their lack of admiration for a preacher. To be called "Rev" or "Preacher" was the last thing needed by an adolescent boy of fragile ego struggling to be "in" with those regarded as "in."

However, I was pleased years later, after I had almost completed my career as a preacher, to have the connection between my life and the preacher of my grandmother's book resurface, and in a surprising and confirming way. It happened in Cullman, Alabama, where I was engaged in a preaching-teaching event at the invitation of First Christian Church (Disciples of Christ). I think the year was 2005—but, if it was, in fact, 2004, who cares? My slippage is not life threatening. A feature of that event in Cullman was a luncheon for ministers from the city and across the state. It was a pleasant occasion, with everyone present being pleasantly surprised to see someone else present. One of my several surprises was the attendance of Robert and Kay Stegall, who I thought were still ministering in Little Rock. They were newly retired and happily at home in Florence, a nearby city. Robert and Kay were natives of my hometown, Humboldt, Tennessee, and so we had a bit of catching up to do. In the context of our banter—half-news, half-gossip—our conversation took a most surprising turn.

"Oh, Dr. Craddock, I have a book that belongs to you," said Kay. "It's in my purse. Just a minute." She quickly returned with her purse. "I'm glad I remembered to bring it; I intended to. When we were packing to move from Little Rock I came across a small box of books, which had been in the front closet for several years. A neighbor who had retired and was returning to Kentucky brought them by, explaining that since they were religion books they might be of interest to us. I thanked her, put the box in the closet and forgot them until we ourselves were packing to move. Only this one interested me. I showed it to Bob and he said you might know of it." At that moment she handed me a small, dark, and obviously old book. The title: *Fred Brenning*. It was *the* book.

Bob and Kay, sharing with me hometown, home church, home schools, knew me as Brenning and my father as Fred. A book bearing both names would surely be important or at least of interest to me. They accepted my fumbling words of amazement and gratitude as I related a brief version of the role of the book in the life of my family, even though neither I nor my father had ever actually seen the book. Kay said, "I'm glad I saved the book; now it is yours." Bob said, "I tried to read it, but, frankly, another story of a boy growing up to be preacher did not interest me." A few more minutes of giving and receiving gratitude and we said our goodbyes.

This had to be the book, but, of course, I had to examine it carefully, to read it, to be absolutely sure that this was the book that moved my grandmother and that gave my father his name and me mine. *A True Story for Boys* was the subtitle, Timothy Trimmer the author. The copy I held was from the seventh printing. The date was 1877; my father was born in 1888. It was published in Nashville, Tennessee, for the Methodist Episcopal Church, South. On the back of the title page there is a note from the editor which reads, in part: "The Author, in making us acquainted with Fred Brenning, writes about a religion that was experienced and enjoyed—about a call to preach that stirred the soul as with the voice of God—about a young itinerant's trials that must have been felt to have been so well described."

It is not likely that you will ever see this book or read it; that is not a matter of importance to either of us. It might, however, be of interest to you that several facts from the life and ministry of Fred Brenning bear a striking resemblance to the life and ministry of Fred Brenning Craddock. For example, Fred Brenning was "noticeably short in stature"; I am 5' 4" on a good day. Or again, Fred Brenning was a product of Sunday school; I was more influenced by Sunday school teachers than by preachers. Or again, Fred Brenning began his ministry in the Southern Appalachians; so did I. Again, Fred Brenning began as an "Exhorter"; so did I. (An Exhorter was something of an apprentice preacher, whose usual duty was to listen to the sermon and then exhort the congregation to live out the message presented. Sometimes the Exhorter prepared the listeners for the sermon by teaching an appropriate lesson from the Bible. On some occasions, often created by emergencies, the Exhorter preached.) Fred Brenning's first preaching station was in a village called Oak Post; mine was in a village called Post Oak.

I will not bother you further with more resemblances, coincidences, and parallels. I need a little time to ponder.

"I will go, sir," was his prompt reply.   (Page 18.)

FRED BRENNING:

A TRUE STORY FOR BOYS.

BY TIMOTHY TRIMMER.

———————
SEVENTH THOUSAND.
———————

Nashville, Tenn.:
PUBLISHED BY A. H. REDFORD, Agent,
FOR THE M. E. CHURCH, SOUTH.
1877.

2

If You Will Let Him Live

I will talk with you later about my relationship with my father. At this point I want simply to say that I do not recall receiving a clear response from him at any time in the decision process of my becoming a preacher. I was perhaps sixteen, near seventeen, when first I felt stirrings toward the pulpit. One Sunday afternoon I privately shared with my father the movement of my mind and heart in that direction. He listened and then cautioned me that the decision was a big one and that I should not be too much influenced by heartwarming youth rallies or worship services. I told him I would take my time; I wanted to be sure. He said simply, "Good, son," and we left it at that.

What did I want from him? Approval? Confirmation? Hallelujah? Maybe I was seeking help in deciding, or maybe I wanted him to decide for me. I don't know. Maybe he was disappointed. He was in the army in World War I and now sons number one and number two were in World War II as airman and sailor. Did son number three considering the ministry translate as wimpy and avoiding his first duty? I don't know. When I was closer to certainty as to call, I told him.

He shook my hand, looked at me with emotion-filled eyes, and said not a word. Several times my mother assured me, "Of course your Daddy is pleased and proud of you; he just has a hard time expressing his feelings." Later, when I was at home on recess from school, he had been drinking. He welcomed me with, "Well, son, don't be like John the Baptist." "How's that?" "Don't lose your head." I needed more from him. I must acknowledge that I did on more than one occasion overhear my father responding to, "Well, Fred, I know you are proud of your namesake becoming a preacher," with good cheer and apparent gratitude. Who can know another's heart?

With Momma it was different; she opened her heart. However, I don't want to mislead you: her faith in God was deep but modest in expression. Her prayers were silent. She was not one to pray and then advertise her prayers; that God heard, of that she had no doubt, was sufficient. When I say, "Momma opened her heart," I do not mean unreservedly; with me, as with my siblings, she seemed to take the measure of my capacity to hear, to receive, to understand, and to bear what she said. She "tempered the wind to the shorn lamb." In this sense she was much like a good rabbi who gives one answer to the beginning student, another to the same student a year later, and another when the student has matured to the point of being a colleague of the rabbi. She knew children could ask questions beyond their ability to deal with a full answer. Curiosity often far outruns mental and emotional capacity. Her answers to my first questions about Santa Claus were at the time adequate; a year later they were inadequate, as she well knew, and so new answers were given.

I recall when first I mentioned to her my "thinking about," "wondering about," "considering as an option," "no commitment, mind you," the ministry. I was about sixteen, maybe seventeen. We were in the kitchen; she was preparing supper. I half expected her to embrace what I said and to embrace me: "That's wonderful, son." She didn't. She turned back to the sink, apparently fully engaged with a head of cabbage. I moved slightly to see her face in order to interpret her silence. She was crying, her tears too full to be a response to a son's vocational probing. Soon she cleared her face and voice and asked, "Have you been reading your Bible?" "Yes, ma'm." "And praying?" "Yes, ma'm." "Then you will make the right decision." I did not expect the tears or the reserve in her response. "I hope so," I said. She had given me more than Daddy, but not enough, or so I thought at the time. Perhaps I wanted from both a clear answer with which I could disagree or agree, but the clear impression that ministry was *my* decision was not welcome. I realize now that God sometimes calls a person in a voice not loud enough for the whole family to hear, but a little confirmation would relieve an adolescent mind.

Of course, teenagers don't have to make life decisions immediately, but for some reason, I felt I had to "Yes" or "No" the ministry so I could feel free again. My siblings and friends talked almost casually about options and preferences as to careers, but with no evident sense of urgency. Not so with me. I did not then nor do I now know whether the burden of choice was a trait of personality, a kind of super-conscientiousness, whether the calling to ministry itself carried a weight, a burden, peculiar to the task itself. Rightly or wrongly, when I thought of possibly becoming a journalist, that would be a choice, 100 percent mine. When I considered becoming a minister that was not totally my decision; I was responding to God's will for me. Of course, I had been told that journalists, lawyers, teachers, merchants, farmers—all could understand their lives as a vocation, a calling, but what I am telling you is that I perceived, I felt, I experienced the idea of being a preacher as different, and that difference was sobering, even burdensome. That's why advice about not being in a hurry, taking my time, was not helpful even if wise. If it was my decision, why could I not make it now; if it was God's decision, why did not God tell me, or at least tell my father or my mother? I prayed for the ache to leave me.

After the brief and less than satisfying conversation in the kitchen with my mother, it occurred to me that I was putting pressure on myself by frequently exposing myself to God talk and God referencing. Maybe I was beginning to overdose on the Christian faith. After all, I was every week in Sunday school, in worship, in youth meetings, in midweek services of prayer and Bible study. No wonder I was thinking so much about ministry; with all that exposure to religion, even Al Capone would begin to feel called to preach. Solution? It was simple; back off from God, from God's influences, from God's people.

My withdrawal plan was simple: sleep late on Sunday morning. That immediately eliminated Sunday school and worship, leaving room in my mind to entertain other ideas and in my schedule to make a few more not so "churchy" friends. Sleeping late on Sunday meant getting past Momma. My excuse worked; I was tired. I had taken an after-school and all-day Saturday job at a general grocery as clerk and clean-up boy. Cleaning up on Saturday night meant I often got home near midnight. "But Momma, I'm tired" was no flimsy, groundless excuse; it was true. Every week bringing home some groceries from the store, and leaving all my pay except for one dollar on the kitchen table tended to give positive reinforcement to my excuse. Not that such acts on my part were offered or received as bribery. I am here offering a long after-the-fact interpretation. To attempt to bribe my mother was not ever for me a possibility; for her to accept a bribe was inconceivable.

The other church gatherings at which I had formerly been faithful became hit and miss, with a variety of excuses appertaining thereto. My plan was working. Although thoughts of being a preacher still visited me more often that I welcomed, the idea was not a burdensome preoccupation. And I had a number of friends who gave no thought to church, much less ministry. In fact, had they known my mind they would have drowned me in laughter.

But my plan soon collapsed under the weight of two factors. One, on a Sunday morning during the summer before my senior year in high school, Momma underscored her weekly call to get up for Sunday school and worship with firm taps on bony parts of my body with a huge table spoon. My toes and shoulder blades capitulated and I was resurrected. Two, absence from church services did not effectively quiet the voice or voices within. The struggle did not return; it never really left.

A number of influences, not one alone decisive but together quite persuasive, moved in and through my life with cumulative effect. They brought enough clarity for me to say "Yes" to God. About these influences I will speak to you in due season. Let me now simply fast-forward about a year. I have graduated from Humboldt High School, have worked in a factory for the summer in order to supply the beginning needs of a college student, and now stand in the kitchen with my mother as she prepares supper. It is Sunday afternoon prior to my catching a bus the next morning.

"Momma, do you remember our conversation in this kitchen over a year ago, when I first mentioned to you that I was 'sort of thinking about being preacher'?"

"Yes, I remember."

"Then you probably also remember that I felt the conversation seemed incomplete, not really satisfying to me."

"Not to me either."

"Why?"

"Because I could not tell you then what I can tell you now."

And the following is my memory of what she told me on the evening before I left for college to begin preparation for seminary and for ministry.

When I was about eight months old I contracted diphtheria. It was in the winter of 1928–29. As you may know diphtheria was a killer of babies and children. Visit old cemeteries and if you find a number of stones marking the graves of children, stones bearing dates within the same period of twelve to eighteen months, you would be safe in guessing that diphtheria had moved across the area and taken away its children. At the first fear of the disease, all children in the family and in the community were told sternly, "Don't go near the baby." Then came all the home remedies volunteered by grandparents, aunts, and uncles. Remedies wrapped in moaning prayers. Were I to recite the concoctions poured into the throat of the child, your response would be "Well. That would be enough to kill the baby." Vinegar, honey, homemade whiskey, kerosene, sugar, seltzer—all in various combinations and around the clock. "Give him a sedative so he can sleep." "No, don't let him sleep. As long as he is crying and coughing the diphtheria cannot smother him." This disease formed a membrane over the air passages to and from the lungs. If the membrane completely covers the air passages, breathing stops and the child dies struggling.

Momma said the remedies were not working; my breathing became increasingly labored. A medical doctor had to be found. If you are thinking this should have been done at the onset of the disease, you are right. But remember the year is 1928–29. Remember the confidence of rural people in tried and true remedies. Remember doctors cost money, a very scarce commodity in this case. Remember doctors were few, and miles away. Remember there was no hospital, even at a distance. To say, "Get a doctor," meant desperation and fear; all else has failed.

There was a telephone about a mile away. Daddy ran the mile. There was a doctor five miles away. He had a telephone. The operator connected Daddy and the doctor. The doctor had recently traded his horse and buggy for a Ford automobile. He was there in a slow flash. His name was Dr. Penn.

Momma said Dr. Penn attended to me with his best medicine, his best methods, and his most comforting words. She said he hummed "Blessed Assurance" the entire night. He was still humming it years later when I went to his small office complaining of sinus congestion. The old gospel tune was apparently sufficient for what ailed you.

As the night wore on, my breathing came with increasing difficulty. Each breath was a rattling gasp. I was growing worse in spite of Dr. Penn's bag of cures, his repeated application, his effort to be reassuring, and "Blessed Assurance." Momma refused to leave the room, in spite of the doctor's insistence. She needed rest and could not rest. Besides, leaving the room would be giving up. Dr. Penn gave me a shot, Momma said, with the look of a doctor who had reached the extreme of his ministry to me. Momma said that at this point the doctor's firm insistence and the unbearable noise of my struggle to breathe drove her from the room. "I will sit with him until daybreak," he assured her.

Momma did not go into the next room where Daddy already sat, upright and sleepless. She left the house and went to the barn, hoping the distance of about one hundred yards would be beyond earshot of my choking. It was not. She lay on loose hay, crying and praying. Her prayer, she said, was, "Dear God, if you will let him live, I will pray every day that he will serve you as a minister." The endless repetition of this prayer relaxed her and she went to sleep.

Daylight slanted between the rough boards of the old barn and waked her. She heard no sounds from the house. She ran. As she rushed into the room, Dr. Penn stirred from a half-sleep. He answered the question she had not formed: "The crisis is over; he is sleeping." Thank you, Dr. Penn. Thank you, God. Handing my mother a few bottles with instructions, he assured her, "He'll be all right, but don't hesitate to call if you need me." With that, he closed his kit, put on coat and hat, and Daddy cranked his Ford, successful on the first turn, "We will pay you, Doctor, when we can." "I know you will. I will send you a bill." How much was it? Don't know; he never sent it. "Blessed Assurance."

Needless to say, I was deeply moved by the story. But I still had a question: "Why didn't you tell me this when we talked last year?" "Well, I guess there are two reasons. In the first place, I felt guilty for bargaining with God. We should not try to use prayer to bargain with God. It's disrespectful. I hope you never do what I did, even if you are desperate as I was. But the main reason I did not tell you until now is that I didn't want you to become a minister because you knew I was praying for you to become one. That would be like your being a minister to please me. It's nice for children to want to please their parents, but not like this. It is too important. I wanted you to say "Yes" to God, not to me."

Momma was probably right. Knowing all the hardships she had suffered, I would have done anything to give her some happiness, even become a preacher. I'm glad she did not tell me of her daily petition until she was sure that God, not I, had answered her prayer. God had answered both our prayers; of that we were both sure. At that moment we could not have been happier.

3

The Midwife

What I am about to say to you is not a parenthesis, a bit of information about my beginning, interesting but not of the fabric of my life. On the contrary, the midwife at my birth and the births of my four siblings was ingredient to the shaping of my mind and heart. From the outset of this project I have intended to speak of her; otherwise I could not connect the dots.

The midwife at my birth on the morning of April 30, 1928, was Nicey Rounds. She was probably in her late fifties at the time. Nicey was African American. I mention this not because you might think it an oddity that at a critically important moment in the life of a southern white family, the birth of a child, the central figure was a black woman. She did not come, perform her service, and leave. Nicey was in and out of our house, in but not out of our lives when no one was being born. She brought with her not only her own particular wisdom and opinions, but she also brought traditions and culture from a world not my own, and for that I remain in her debt. In fact, there were three African American families who influenced my formation in ways both subtle and apparent. I speak of it at this

21

point in this narration of the early years because the influences were radically modified later. We did not drift apart; we were separated by public school. We continued as neighbors and friends, but separate schools and later separate churches pulled us apart in spite of ourselves.

I said there were three African American families influential in my formation; let me tell you about them. I begin with the Hunts, Will and Mary, because they were the oldest. Of course, to a child a person of forty would be old, but the Hunts were really old. They had great-grandchildren my age. On one of our walks I asked Will how old he was. "I don't rightly know," he said. "They say I was born during that long dry spell." Good enough. Mary was overweight, happy, and always cooking. She addressed every situation with food. That suited me just fine. When I passed her house on the way to school, she would be on the porch with food: sausage and biscuit, boiled egg, baked sweet potato—something to supplement the lunch I carried. It was always something I could put in my pocket and nibble on "during books." Mary would laugh and say, "If the teacher catches you, tell her to talk to me. A starving boy can't do his numbers or do his reading." On occasion I ate with Will and Mary at their table. My only attempt to eat possum was at their table. Awful. Momma always said to eat what is set before you, but I couldn't. Mary laughed and took away the possum.

Mary stayed in the house; her feet were broken down. But Will was always outside, splitting stove wood, cutting weeds, feeding his pigs, tending his garden. I helped him sometimes, but mostly I joined him on his walks. He could neither read nor write but he was wise, and my teacher. It was Will, not my schoolteacher, who taught me to place a broom straw on a watermelon and if the straw turned a full revolution, the melon was ripe. It was Will, not my schoolteacher, who taught me that grape vines cling to trees because they are scared. When the Almighty was creating everything, he forgot to warn the garden of Eden, "Tomorrow I am making an elephant." When the elephant ran by the grapevine, the vine was scared and held onto a tree. "See?" said Will, "it's still holding tight." And it was. Will knew when fox grapes ripened, and possum grapes, and muscadines. "Don't take more than you can eat; the Almighty wants us to share with the animals." "Will, why can't I stay home from school and let you be my teacher?" "Because you want to learn what's in the books and Will can't read them to you." There was a sadness in him, and I felt it. But he cheered up and so did I, quickening our pace toward Mary's warm bread and cold milk.

The Graves family—John, Jeanetta, and their two sons—were very different from the Hunts. They were younger: the younger son, J. W., was my age; his brother, Lee Grant, was probably eight or ten years older. John and Jeanetta had attended public school, read the newspaper, listened to news on the radio, and had informed opinions on what was going on in the world. They did not shuffle and stare at their shoelaces in the presence of white folk. They were our closest neighbors; our families borrowed from each other; we were frequently in each other's home; J. W. was my playmate. He laughed at me for being so white, I laughed at him for being so black. We were an alibi for each other when our mothers sought the source of mischief. We snickered and laughed lying in the grass, dreaming of our futures. I promised to vote for him if he wanted to be president, a dream shot out of the sky by another neighbor: "A black can't be president." "Why?" "Because he's black."

Jeanetta hated black-white tensions. "That should have been settled by the war," she would say. "The war" was the Civil War, continued in the stares, on the tongues, in the hearts, and occasionally with acts of violence. Jeanetta wanted peace and at times tried to initiate reconciliation, with little success. Even John tried to hush her, saying "Give it time, honey." It was she who named their firstborn Lee Grant, the two names symbolizing reconciliation. Rather than softening anger, pronouncing his name inflamed it. I rode once into town with Lee Grant, sitting beside him in the wagon. Curses and threats and stones were hurled at us. We hurried home, afraid and confused. I did not speak of it, even to Momma, for a long time. I am sure Jeanetta was deeply hurt if Lee Grant told her about the abuse in town, but I doubt that he did. Boys don't like to hurt their mothers. The pain I carried because of the Graves family was different from the sadness over Will Hunt's illiteracy, but the pain and sadness return, with anger, even now as I speak to you about it.

Now, back to the midwife. My relation to her also brought pain but it was quite different. In her case, the pain was wrapped in mystery involving the supernatural. In fact, I was so awed by her power that I did not even think she felt pain; she overpowered pain. At least, so I thought until years later, but by then she was dead.

Were Nicey Rounds only a midwife, commentary on her would be brief, and influence on my life would be nil. A midwife comes to the home having been notified that birth was impending. In the absence of a medical doctor she cared for the mother, aided the delivery, cared for the baby. She attended to both for hours or days, depending on complications, and then left the home. Five times Nicey so served our family. As a four-and-a-half-year-old, I have a few vague memories of her service at the birth of Roland. I remember her assumption of authority: "Bring in water from the well"; "Keep the fire going in the stove"; "Go play outside"; "Don't disturb your mother"; "Keep the door closed"; "Fix yourself a sandwich"; "Don't ask so many questions." We obeyed. Momma said, "Do what Nicey says. She is in charge." Boy, was she in charge! Not loud, not militant, not edgy, just firm in word and confident in manner. I can see her still: exercising full authority as though we were in her house. Daddy stayed out of the way, as did the cat and the dog, and even the chickens—which ran free in the yard—gave her wide berth.

Nicey lived in the area; I would often see her coming and going, never loitering, always moving as on a mission. In fact, she often came to our house when no midwife duties were in order. She visited with Momma, checked on "her children," and then proceeded to take a few things: a jar of jelly or home-canned beans, a slice of fat back pork, and sometimes a live chicken. She did not behave as a thief nor was she regarded as such; she acted as though she was taking what was her own. I did not understand, I did not protest, I did not ask any questions. I simply wondered.

Needless to say, I was fascinated by Nicey, perhaps even awed. Who was she? What was the source of her confidence, her personality power? She had a family. I never knew of a Mr. Rounds, but she had a son Robert, and a grandson Robert Jr. He was my age, but we did not play together. I seldom saw him, and, when I did, he was alone. He seemed to have no childhood. We reentered each other's lives as teenagers. He had by that time become a ball of flaming rage. I will tell you why in a few minutes.

Nicey Rounds had her power in the realm of the supernatural. In saying this I do not mean that she subscribed to the popular "good luck–bad luck" superstitions: salt tossed over the left shoulder; a piece of fat meat under the front step; an open umbrella in the house; enter one door, exit another; and countless others. I never recall her speaking of any of them. What I do recall was her telling me sternly to be sure the cover was replaced over the well after drawing water. If the well is uncovered after dark, "they will come up out of the well," she warned. If they come out, they will destroy until daybreak, burning a barn, spoiling meat in the smokehouse, sickening a child, or killing a cow. One night I bolted upright in bed, remembering that I had failed to return the cover over the well. Even though I was afraid of the dark, I went out and replaced the cover. For days I waited in fear, expecting to hear of a tragedy in the community. In time I convinced myself that I had successfully capped the well; they had not come from the underworld into my world. As I now reflect on it, I probably believed in demons before I believed in God.

On another occasion, Nicey walked rather hurriedly past me when I was playing. She so dominated the scene that

I cannot remember with whom I was playing—perhaps my brothers. I stopped playing and ran after her.

"Where are you going?"

"I am going to Mr _____'s place."

"Is someone having a baby?"

"No, I am going to put a curse on his garden."

"What will happen to his garden?"

"It will wither and die."

"Why are you doing it?"

"Because he called me 'an old nigger.'"

I was afraid because I had no doubt she had the power.

Following the event I will now relate, Nicey Rounds moved out of my small world and I never saw her again. Her departure was unrelated to me except it left me with many unanswered questions; her absence was very real. I cannot reconstruct the time frame; I can only say that I was in the beginning years of public school. I know that Robert Jr. and I had been separated by the segregated school system, but a tragic turn of events separated from my world the entire Rounds family.

Robert Rounds was arrested and charged with theft and murder. He confessed to the theft but denied the murder. He confessed that one wintry night he took a burlap bag and stole several lumps of coal from a pile behind a small grocery. Coal was at a premium; one lump in a stove or fireplace multiplied the heat in the room and could make happy a whole family. My brother and I often walked the railroad tracks, picking up pieces of coal that fell from the locomotive. Coal had replaced wood as fuel. The coal pile behind the small general store was a temptation too strong for Robert. The store was near my home; I was often sent to it to by my mother, and sometimes went on my own when a penny fell my way. The story circulating was this: Robert went to steal coal, but his action disturbed a dog, which wakened the owner. Discovered and frightened, Robert shot the approaching grocer.

But did Robert kill the grocer? The jury said "yes" even though no gun was found nor was it established that Robert owned a gun. A neighbor to the grocer did respond to the noise that night and did fire his gun in the direction of the robbery. But both the grocer and his neighbor were white; Robert was black, and that was the governing fact at the trial, according to my parents. Robert was sentenced to life in prison. My confusion never was able to form any but emotional questions. Later, when I encountered Robert Jr., we were in our teens and able to talk about his father. Robert Jr. and his mother had moved to town, where she worked the rest of her life as a domestic. He was bitter with a generalized anger against all whites. When I told him that my family thought his father innocent of murder, he said that many folks said that, but his father still went to prison. Robert Jr. vented his hatred of white people and once wanted to fight me. Shortly after that painful episode, he decided to catch a freight train to visit his father. He fell under the moving train, a leg was severed, and he bled to death. I visited his mother but she never said a word. A tragic sequence of events thus had no conclusions.

But where was Nicey? I wanted to talk with her even though I probably would have been unable to do so. What would I say? I was a frightened, sensitive child; she was a powerful woman who knew so much and was in league with supernatural beings. She worked with demons; of that I had been persuaded. But where was she and what was she doing? Her son was convicted falsely and sat in a distant prison cell. If she could curse the garden of a white man who called her a "nigger," what would she do to all the whites who had conspired against her son? Surely in her repertoire of incantations there was a curse that would address the crime against her family, unleashing the full fury of her revenge. I expected as much and waited to hear the horrible news of burning barns, dying livestock, sick babies, and withered gardens.

Nothing happened beyond the usual accidents and illnesses. I was relieved but also surprised. Had she lost her power? Surely she had not abandoned her son and her son's son. "Has anyone seen Nicey?" I enquired at random, in and out of the family, but received only negative replies with guesses: maybe she is ill; maybe she moved; maybe she is ashamed because of Robert. I successfully concealed the depth of my anxiety and concern. When I asked Robert Jr. several years later about his grandmother, he angrily said, "What do you care?" I told him she was midwife in my family, delivering my sister, my three brothers, and me. He said she had died. When? Several years ago.

I cannot tell you any more. I wish I could, but my memory comes up empty. Not that I have forgotten her; as you can see, I have not. I would like to know more of her power. Did it work to reward or only to punish? Was her power given to her or did she discover she had it all along? If given, did she understand it was from God? If demons are real, was God real to her as well? Or was she simply playing with the mind of a little white boy? Whatever is the truth, my experience of Nicey Rounds gave impetus and urgency to questions about God, which I soon would be able to ask. I suppose you could say Nicey pushed me into theology. I could live with her absence, but not with silence. Someone would have to fill the silence and answer my questions about race, justice, deep hatred, and the world of demons. In other words, questions about God.

And why didn't I share my fears and anxieties with my siblings? I don't know. Why not with my parents? I don't know. Why did I live so much inside myself? I don't know. Was not life too much, too complex, too painful to bear alone? Yes. Then why so private? I don't know.

I think I need now to talk to you about my parents.

4

My Mother

My mother was born Ethel Marie Hood on November 8, 1900, in rural Haywood County, Tennessee, in the community of Tibbs, near Nut Bush. The Hood family lived on a small farm, which provided for a family of two girls and three boys, Marie or "Ree" being the youngest. The Hoods had moved into West Tennessee from Kentucky. Whether Gen. John Bell Hood, also of Kentucky, was related to my maternal ancestors, I do not know. My maternal grandmother, the only one of my grandparents I was privileged to know, was a Stevenson, descended from John Stevenson of County Antrim, Ireland. John came to America to fight in the revolution against England; he is buried in Whitfield County, Georgia.

In the family and in the community Marie was often referred to as "Baby Sister," even after she was grown and married. The term referred not only to her being the last-born but also to the way the family related to her. Momma admitted to being "babied"; she was small (five feet tall as an adult), pretty, and privileged in the eyes of her siblings. Years later, when her sister and brother visited in our home, evidence of her being spoiled was clear. But none of the small favors along the way of her growing up weakened her; she proved herself able to handle with grace and patience what turned out to be a life of hardship.

Momma remembered her childhood as simple, happy, and ordinary. She learned in the home how to be a homemaker, and in the fields she learned harvest labor. She, like other girls of her station, wore a bonnet and long sleeves to protect her skin from the sun. Girls did not want to go to church or to parties with the brown skin of field hands. She graduated from the local school after eight years of study. To go beyond the eighth grade would mean travel and tuition. Few students did so, especially the females. In fact, some of the teachers in the local school had only an eighth grade education. Momma herself was a substitute teacher, never losing her appetite for learning. She helped her own children with homework when they were high schoolers. Regardless of requirements of school, in our home it was required that we use proper grammar, spelling, and diction. And Daddy reenforced this expectation with his own example.

Life in rural Haywood County in the early 1900s revolved around family, school, and church. There was not much distance among the three: Bible reading and prayer joined family and church: memory exercises at school included Bible verses. Teachers in school and in church were often the same. Church buildings and school buildings were also community centers. The same persons attended worship services and square dances, and, of course, everyone prepared for and attended the county fair, competing with friendly fierceness for blue ribbons in foods, needlework, and animal husbandry. The dance at the close of the fair was the icing on the cake. Young women and young men looked, smiled, waited, hoped, and danced. It was at a Haywood County Fair that Marie Hood met a young man from Gibson County, Fred Craddock. He had entered his horse, Bob Taylor, in the trotter's race. His horse did not win the race but he won the heart of Marie.

It is important for my purpose in writing that you meet my mother, but it is especially important that you meet her in the church of her upbringing. The Hoods were Methodists and Marie was baptized in that tradition and brought up in its worship, creed, and moral instruction. Her childhood and youth preceded the denominational merger creating the United Methodist Church. Strictly speaking, Marie belonged to the Methodist Episcopal Church, South, but even that does not define her religiously. It is common knowledge that within the same denomination congregations differ widely. There may be as much difference between rural and urban Methodist churches as between Methodists and Presbyterians within the same culture. Marie belonged to a congregation that was Methodist as defined in a rather remote, small, tightly knit, family-centered, southern farm community. To that congregation the annual conference sent a preacher to lead a worship service one Sunday afternoon per month. That brief visit by a preacher, usually young and inexperienced, was hardly a defining feature in the ongoing life, belief system, and social practices of the community. The *King James Bible,* the Apostles Creed, and the hymns of the Wesley brothers, all as understood for generations, gave definition and continuity to Christianity in the community of Tibbs.

One would expect, therefore, that young Marie would be formed religiously in the likeness of parents and peers, and to a large extent this was the case. When I asked her years later about the contours of the Christian life according to the church and home of her youth, Momma spoke of living simply and sharing with those less fortunate. She spoke of modest dress, clean speech, avoiding bad habits, abstaining from tobacco and alcohol, respect for the elderly, Bible reading, and prayer. Hymns were sung in the home. She often accompanied them on the guitar or harmonica. The Bible was accepted as the inspired word of God, but most attention was given to the teaching and example of Jesus. She did not regard her upbringing as being in any way unusual. Her family's Methodism was conservative Wesleyan piety.

But where in this description is the wellspring that gave birth to and nourished her strong sense of social justice? Was she disturbed by the social and economic inequities in her world, especially as evident in black-white relationships? Maybe one of the frequent revivals at her church brought an evangelist who stirred her awake to social ills in the world. Or maybe the time she spent with the gospel stories of Jesus were fuel enough to create a discontent with the way things were in her world and the larger society. There were newspapers in the home, and a radio; she was politically aware. I cannot locate the sources of her growth in grace. I do know that in 1920 women in the country were permitted to vote and that in the first presidential election in which she could vote she cast her ballet for Norman Thomas, the Socialist Party candidate. I was shocked to learn this and asked her why: "Momma, you were close to being a Communist!" Her reply was that Norman Thomas was the candidate most concerned for the poor, for the plight of children, for the neglect of the elderly in our society. To my mother, the primary duty of government was to care for those unable to care for themselves. She never wavered from this conviction. As long as anyone is hungry or ill, the worst social sins were waste and greed. For example, she voted against air-conditioning the church building; she voted against buying pew cushions. Jesus, she said, would have us spend that money to feed and clothe. Simple living enables one to give generously.

Momma was not what you might call a political activist. She did not march. In her mind Jesus' Sermon on the Mount could become national policy if all Jesus' followers would vote their faith. In fact, she did not talk her religion very much, even in the home. Through her life and in her quiet ways, her children, her friends, and her neighbors were all made aware of "the way of Jesus." I never recall her quoting or referring to Paul's letters or any of the New Testament other than the gospels. She never distinguished among the four gospels; to her they were one story of what Jesus said and what Jesus did.

And she never was persuaded to use any translation other than the *King James*. When I began study for the ministry, I went home at Christmas. She was impressed that I was beginning to read Hebrew and Greek, but my *Revised Standard Version* of the Bible with its maroon cover did not impress her. "What's wrong with the Bible I gave you?" was her only comment.

In light of what I have said about Momma, it is probably no surprise to learn she was a pacifist. My father had been a soldier during World War I but I never heard them argue about war. They were 180 degrees apart but I never heard one try to persuade the other. Not even in that painful time in the early 1940s when my two older brothers went to war; one in the Army, the other in the Navy. Their enlistment prompted pride in Daddy, tears in Momma. It was not uncommon to slip into the kitchen for milk and cookies and find her working and crying at the sink. She had nightmares and visions of her sons in danger. Many mothers did, but her pacifism, her deep abhorrence of violence, made her anxieties doubly painful. No flag waving, no patriotic speeches offered relief. But her pacifism pertained not only to the military and to war; she reminded me continually of peaceful resolutions of all tension and potential violence. There is never an excuse.

"But what was I to do?"

"Jesus said to turn the other cheek."

"But if I do that, every boy at school will want to fight me."

"You don't know that; they may learn from your example and no one will want to fight."

"Fat chance."

"Following Jesus is not easy, but it is the path you have chosen."

"Yes ma'am."

Momma knew that Daddy was taking me aside with different advice on how to respond to bullies, but she never wavered. As I matured I stood closer to her than to him. Arguments for a just war have always been for me almost but not quite persuasive. There is, of course, a major difference between two boys on a schoolyard and two nations in hostile postures. Even so, Momma placed indelibly before me the beckoning of a nonviolent Jesus.

I do not want to give the impression that Momma's pacifism immobilized her, making her cautious and careful not to say or do anything with which someone might disagree or to which there might be a negative reaction. Her piety was filled with initiatives appropriate to the range of her opportunities to meet needs. Her world was as large as could be reached by walking. She did not drive, but, then, we had no car. In her youth she had her own horse and side saddle. Now as wife and mother she had access to a buggy and old Bess, but old Bess was usually busy pulling farm machinery, sometimes harnessed with old Red, our mule. We boys rode old Bess sometimes, but without the benefit of a saddle. So Momma walked. She walked to homes when there was illness, an accident, a new baby, a crisis; no difference was made between black and white, prosperous or pauper. She went when someone came to "fetch Miss Marie"; she went when no one sent for her. She even attended to a cranky old man down the road who shot our dog.

"Why help him? Besides, he's crazy."

"He is not crazy; he is an epileptic."

"Well, he killed our dog."

"I know, but he still needs help sometimes."

She talked with and often fed hoboes who jumped on and off freight cars on the L and N rail line near our house. She helped neighbors process meat after killing hogs. Sometimes we complained that she put others ahead of us, but she didn't really. She served, cooked, kept house, nursed us through childhood illnesses, and tried to keep the house warm in winter. But we needed to know, she said, that it is not enough just to care for your own family.

She repeated that conviction when she brought persons into our home, for various reasons, for varying lengths of time. A young woman with a baby, unwelcome in her own family, was welcome in ours. For how long? I don't remember. A teenage boy whose mother died. For how long? Maybe a year. An old man who fell from a wagon while drunk, breaking a leg. He had no one to care for him. Momma did; he was in our home six months. The thing is, we didn't have room. While we were on the farm, our home had two regular beds, a child's bed, and a crib. There were seven of us; you do the math. When we moved to town, we were pressed into a small square house: living room, kitchen, two bedrooms. There were still seven of us, sometimes eight, sometimes nine. Don't try to do the math; this calls for geometry. My brother Alvin told friends at school we had moved into a four-bedroom house; we slept in four rooms! But Momma and Daddy kept a sense of humor and found something funny in every day's impossibilities. On more than one occasion, when a radio brought music into our house, we saw our parents dance among the beds. Those were the salad days, but I didn't know it at the time. I must say, however, that Momma with her music and Daddy with his stories cushioned us from the cold edge of poverty.

Momma was a musician, without any training. She just "picked it up." A little while with any instrument and she could play it. The only instrument she owned was a small harmonica, but with it she blessed the house with hymns and old favorites. Years later, almost too late, I brought her from Germany a Hohner harmonica. With it she could quiet a room with "Danny Boy."

When we could no longer make the payments on the small farm, bank officials came with papers and with, I think, genuine regrets. What an awful day. We moved into town (Humboldt) into that little box of a house; rent was $2.00 a week. There was no electricity, no running water. "Let's be thankful we have a roof over our heads" she said. Because of Daddy's drinking, Momma had to be the breadwinner. She got a job at Brown Shoe Company putting Buster Brown stickers inside children's shoes. My siblings and I were getting old enough to pitch in, and we did: cleaning up at the Five and Dime, mowing cemetery lots, delivering the *Memphis Press-Scimitar* and the *Grit*. Within two years we had electricity, a radio, and a used bicycle. We were on our way.

For Momma, the move to town was both a danger and a blessing. It was a danger because in town there were temptations and bad influences. New friends were checked out; pool halls were forbidden territory. If a newspaper customer was in a pool hall, I had to wait until he came out to collect for the paper. She listened for any "ugly words" that slipped into our speech. Her familiar lectures against gambling, smoking, and drinking were now repeated with urgency. Once she said, "If someone held out to you a tablespoon of alcohol and said, 'Drink it and live, refuse it and die,' then tell him to shoot, 'I will not drink it.'" Of course, Daddy's increasing addiction added to her fear that one or more of her children would become alcoholics.

On the other hand, the blessing of town living was access to church. Momma had joined the church to which Daddy already belonged, Central Avenue Christian Church in Humboldt. Many members of the extended Craddock family were instrumental in founding that congregation first in a home and later in an impressive building of its own. Prior to my memory of him, Daddy was regular in attendance, especially in the large Men's Bible Class. He is seen in the old class photographs. Momma was welcome into that congregation and she took her place comfortably in Sunday school, worship Sunday morning and evening, and prayer services on Wednesday evening. In the early years of their marriage Daddy had an automobile and enjoyed some success in farming and small business ventures. As far as I have been able to discover, alcohol was not a problem for him in those days. At this point I need only say that my experience of him was post-prosperity, mid-alcoholism, mid-national Depression. Our family was isolated on the farm, without car or telephone, in heavy debt, and daily aware of the Depression that gripped the nation.

But now we were in town, within walking distance of the church. Women of the Ladies Aid Society visited, brought some used clothing for children, and urged upon Momma what she had already determined to do: get her five children in Sunday school. Sunday school and morning worship ("Do we have to stay for church? It's boring.") were required; evening and mid-week services were urged but not required. Momma went to church often, sometimes without her children, always without Daddy. In my remembrance, he attended on some special occasions perhaps a dozen times. Daddy's griping about Sunday lunch being late hurt Momma but did not deter her. She was determined to raise her children in church and she did. She sat every Sunday on the same pew, placing us around her according to who was and who was not behaving at the time.

Although she sat with us in worship, at other times she served in ways women served in that church: preparing and cleaning up after fellowship meals, preparing and cleaning up communion ware, attending meetings of church women, taking her turn as a Sunday school class officer, passing out class lesson materials, and sending cards to the ill. But in that day, in that church, a woman was never nominated to hold office as a deacon. She did not see herself as put down as a woman, but as serving after the manner of Jesus. In many ways she was very conservative herself, which became most apparent in her expectations of our ministers. They were to read and interpret Scripture texts every Sunday; they were to visit the sick, invite the unchurched, care for the needy, live above reproach, be well spoken of throughout the community, and always dress as becomes men of God. Once she voted against a candidate for the pulpit, a candidate who had thoroughly impressed the congregation with his credentials and abilities. "Mrs. Craddock, why in the world would you vote 'No'?" "He came among us as a guest wearing a bright red tie and he had no hat." Needless to say, he came over her objection. Within six months he was in her opinion the best minister ever, and at his departure three years later, Momma wept.

Momma died at the age of eighty after several years of near helplessness, the victim of several minor strokes and one major one. My sister Frieda cared for her in her home, refusing to place her in a nursing facility. At the time of her death, Momma had been for nineteen years a widow. She had also been preceded in death by her oldest son, William Walter. Her funeral was held in our church, where she was mourned by many, including black friends. If any objected, they said nothing; they knew Momma's mind on the matter.

5

My Father

My father, Fred Brenning Craddock Sr., was born on December 5, 1888, in rural Crockett County, Tennessee, in the family home located on the Collinsworth Levee Road between the towns of Alamo and Humboldt. He had six siblings: one sister and five brothers. He was not the youngest of the lot but he was the last to leave the home. He cared for his parents until their deaths, which occurred only a few months apart. He was a small man, about 5 feet 7 inches and at his heaviest he probably weighted 150 pounds. But he was physically strong. When he finished high school he attended business college in Memphis, where he lived in the YMCA. He participated in the athletic opportunities of the Y, including boxing. He received from his father a gold watch for abstaining from tobacco and alcohol until age twenty-one. Our father taught his sons how to walk correctly so as not to tire, and on many mornings, cold or hot, he had us on the porch doing deep breathing exercises. He remained strong even though he was heavily into tobacco and alcohol in all my memory of him. I saw him chin himself with one arm when he was past fifty years of age. When sober, he was agile and light on his feet. He enjoyed the reputation of being a good dancer in his youth. I can testify to that. More than once, after we reached sufficient prosperity to own a battery radio, I saw Daddy sweep Momma across the floor to the rhythm of some familiar tune. Daddy was thirty-two when he married; Momma was twenty. He was forty when I was born.

Within a year of this writing, my surviving brothers, Alvin (two years older) and Roland (four years younger) and I spent a few days in casual and sometimes meaningless conversation. Mostly we remembered, or tried to do so. Some memories, once painful, we found to be—from the safe distance of age— actually humorous. Laughter exorcised old tears; it was a good time. I remembered Daddy and the mood changed. I learned what I had long suspected; my siblings did not want to talk about Daddy. I already knew that Walter, my oldest brother (deceased), very seldom spoke of him. Walter was a storyteller and writer, and in one of his stories I recognized Daddy but the disguise worked apparently for everyone but me. Frieda, my sister and oldest sibling (deceased), sometimes recalled something funny in Daddy's remembered words. Her relation to Daddy had been closer all along, and that relationship enabled her to think and feel past his alcohol.

It was not so with Alvin and Roland. Every memory of theirs reeked of Daddy's alcohol; his drinking had impoverished and embarrassed the family and each of us had to make our way around him. I could not deny the truth in their painful recollections, but it was evident that I had other memories. My other memories do not erase theirs; I reexperienced a lot of hurt, but my other memories were of the same man. I mentioned but a few; I did not want to try to rewrite family history, or to correct them, or to defend Daddy. After several hours we moved to another subject.

And with you, the reader, I do not wish to appear to be rehabilitating my father. There is no point to that. However, in this effort to identify the streams of influence on my life, especially on the formative years, Daddy is significantly present, and in positive ways. Maybe because I was named for him I looked and listened harder and longer than my siblings. Maybe because I bore his name I was more willing to explain him, even defend him. Maybe I sometimes heard and saw what I wanted to hear and see. If so, accept what I write here as memories and not as chronicles of a disinterested reporter. I know that quite early I recognized the pattern of Daddy's life. There were five movements. First, there was the period of sobriety during which he was present to the family, full of wit, humor, and good stories. Second, there was the beginning of drinking, triggered by nothing more than his addiction, during which he tried to hide his drinking by silence and intermittent observations on the sad state of affairs in the world, local and beyond. Third, drinking had now made Daddy unreasonably happy. His laughter was too loud and inappropriate, he was generous, and behaved as though he were spreading joy in the world. Fourth, Daddy was now angry, filled with generalized hostility, issuing threats and verbal abuse. I recall no physical abuse, although it seemed imminent; all of us steered clear of him until his rage subsided. Fifth and finally, Daddy was ill, physically ill. He shut the door of his bedroom, but we knew by Momma's frequent trips in and out, urging us to be quiet. She gave him paregoric and raw eggs in milk. This stage lasted several days, ending when Daddy returned to the family table, silent except for promises never to drink again. But in and around and through these five movements are scattered memories, good memories, relieving the pain that was his and therefore ours. I am pleased that this effort at recalling has brought them back to me.

I remember small expressions of affection for Momma. I never doubted their love for each other. One evening he came home with a small package, gift-wrapped. He surprised her with it as we sat down for supper. "Fred, you shouldn't have; we are certainly in no shape to be buying gifts." It was a bottle of hand lotion. Momma protested the splurging, but she smiled through tears. Where had he gotten the money? From the Mother's Oats box in which we all put coins to pay the $2.00 per week rent.

Daddy said to us all: "If this family is ever reduced to what goes in and out of that box, we might as well be dead."

I remember the Sunday afternoons when Daddy resolved or dissolved the tensions among us siblings. The tensions developed as in every home: who hit whom first; who got more than his or her share of pie; who was a tattle-tale; whose turn was it to bring in firewood; who said an "ugly word"; who let the dog into the kitchen; who did not play fair. Big issues for small children. Daddy listened for a while, wrote down the time and place of the incident and the persons involved, declared a temporary truce with the promise that these issues would be settled on Sunday afternoon. On Sunday afternoon, he went outside, placed a quilt on the ground, called us together on the quilt, took his list of the week's disputes, and began his role as referee. One by one, the tensions, the times, places, and persons involved were read with instructions on how they were to be resolved: one round or two rounds or three rounds of boxing. The quilt was the boxing ring. But nobody wanted to fight: "I forgot what I was mad about"; "That was a long time ago"; "I'm not angry any more"; "We want to play now"; "It was my fault"; "I'm sorry." I do not recall any fight ever. All shook hands, Daddy declared a draw, tore up his list, picked up the quilt, and went inside. All was well again.

I remember Daddy's stories. As I recall, he did not tell stories that one could read in books, or even stories that were a part of an oral tradition. His stories were original, sometimes created on the spot, but always told as actual events, real experiences. It was this "as though it really happened" quality that disturbed Momma, worrying her that we might grow up unable to distinguish fact from fiction. It was a reasonable concern. I think if he had begun, "Once upon a time," she would trust that we would recognize what followed as an imaginary tale. But he didn't. For example, he might come home in the evening, move to the warmth of the fireplace and say, "I hope I never see again what I saw today." Then he would begin the ritual of rolling and lighting a cigarette. We were trapped in the suspense.

"What did you see today?"

"Oh, you kids still up? I thought it was your mother who came in."

"What did you see?"

"No, you go on to bed; you don't want to have nightmares."

Back and forth it went until he was ready and then, "Well, sit down, but don't blame me if you can't sleep." Or he might begin, "What did you study in school today?" When we answered, he proceeded to supplement our schoolwork with stories of Quantrill, or Chief Loud Thunder, or General Lee, or Abe Lincoln. Until we learned better, we would proudly take our new information to school, certain of receiving extra credit, only to be set down with, "Did your father tell you that?" When I entered first grade, pupils answered roll call on Fridays with a Bible verse. I told Daddy I didn't have a Bible verse and the teacher would give me a poor mark. He told me to sit down; he would teach me a verse. He did. "Samson took the ass bone of a mule and killed ten thousand Filipinos." I recited my verse proudly and without a bobble. Needless to say, the teacher was not happy, reprimanded me, and sent my parents a note expressing her displeasure. Momma: "Fred, how could you?" Daddy: "I'll bet the class enjoyed it." Me: "But it sounded like Bible."

I hope you sense how different my parents were. From this safe distance I can speak in general about how opposites attract and how their differences made life more interesting. But when I recall in some detail the difficulties almost too much for a child, I am again aware of unresolved tensions. It helped a bit for Daddy to say, "Now, kids, always obey your mother," and for Momma to say, "Always respect your father. He loves you."

Daddy loved Christmas because it let his imagination run free. Lack of money kept the usual getting and spending to a minimum, but there was an extravagance in our celebration of Santa Claus. You see, we had more evidence of Santa's existence than did our peers, even those who were laden with gifts. We had more than evidence; we had proof. The object of our observance of Christmas was to catch Santa Claus. During the night before Christmas, strange noises came from the roof. We were roused from sleep and taken outside. We couldn't see, but we had heard. Back inside we were again stirred out of sleep. The snack of milk and cookies left for Santa had been consumed. Need more proof? Again at dawn Daddy gathered us around the fireplace. There in the ashes were two footprints, one print going into the fireplace, the other coming out. Big boots made the prints, bigger than Daddy's, probably as big as Lee Grant's. Let the bigger boys doubt as much as they want; we knew without a doubt, and Daddy already had a plan to catch Santa Claus next year.

Perhaps my best Christmas was the one that seemed the worst until some years later when I learned the mystery of it. The Depression was at its worst; the family purse was empty. I had overheard Momma say to Daddy that there would be no Christmas. There was no way. And yet Christmas morning our shoe boxes, set in a row anticipating Santa, held their annual goodies: an apple in each, a tangerine in each, raisins still on the stem in each, a box of sparklers in each, a packet of Black Cat fire crackers in each. We were in business. Merry Christmas! How did it happen? I had the answer about ten years later. Momma said Daddy used a pair of pliers to pull one of his molars. That molar had a gold crown, put there by an Army dentist during World War I. Daddy removed the crown and went to town where he sold the gold for enough to provide gifts from Santa Claus. Daddy never spoke of it and as long as he lived I kept his secret.

I remember being quarantined with malaria. No one else in the family contracted it. I was miserable: the fever, the sweating, the headaches, the awful quinine, the yellow skin, the days and nights of wondering if I would ever recover. Not the least of my miseries was the isolation. My siblings and friends were playing, and I was piled up in bed. I complained. One of my major whining days brought Daddy into the room. He had in his hand three books, which he tossed on my bed and said in a pleasant but firm voice, "Son, there is no way to modulate the human voice to make a whine acceptable." Feeling both instructed and reprimanded, I pondered his words. I did not know the word *modulate,* but I understood his words and his action: stop whining and read; even bedridden, one can do something constructive. One book was *The Life and Times of Billy Sunday.* Daddy had brought the book home from Camp Gordon in Chamblee, Georgia (now Fort Gordon, near Augusta). Billy Sunday had preached to the soldiers. His life as a professional baseball player and his call to be an evangelist were interesting but I was unable to grasp his sermons. A second book was Momma's Bible, *King James Version.* I read some of it, found its sentences and vocabulary difficult, but kept trying out of respect for Momma who loved it. The third book was *The Complete Works of William Shakespeare.* It was Daddy's book. Reading Shakespeare at age eight and nine? Not with understanding, but I tried. It sounded much like the *King James Bible.* The plays were of a world too strange, but even so, some of the lines stayed in my mind. And years later I found myself reciting some of the sonnets though I do not recall trying to memorize them.

It was Shakespeare, strangely enough, who aided communication between Daddy and me shortly before his death in the Veteran's Hospital in Memphis. He was dying of cancer of the throat. He had been treated with radiation and surgery, leaving him weak, unable to eat, unable to speak, but fully able to feel pain. On a table by his bed was a stack of get-well cards, every one of which came from persons and groups in Central Avenue Christian Church, the church he often criticized and whose ministers he belittled in their efforts to reclaim him. Daddy saw me looking through the cards, and unable to speak, he scribbled on the side of a tissue box a line from *Hamlet:* "In this harsh world draw your breath in pain to tell my story." I wrote, "And what is your story, Daddy?" He wrote, "I was wrong." I did not return to seminary until after his funeral a few days later. The service was held in Central Avenue Christian Church during which the congregation sang his favorite hymn, "When Peace Like a River." Daddy was sixty-three years old.

When the time came to share with the church and with my family that I was clear enough about a call to ministry to begin studies in preparation for it, I was confident that my being a Christian minister would have a life-changing effect on my father. With a son, his own namesake, going into the ministry, would not Daddy toss the bottle forever and return to the pew beside my mother? Surely. But I was naïve, knowing nothing about the power of addiction. In my disappointment, I visited with a vocational counselor. He shocked me with the suggestion that maybe my motivation to be minister was not a call from God but my own desire to reform my father. I have not yet forgotten the pain and the confusion of that session. Were the counselor's words not just a possibility but the truth? I can no longer linger over these recollections; multiplying them will likely shed no more light on my exploration of the network of influences on my finally arriving at the pulpit. It might be appropriate at this point to remind the reader and myself that the dedicatory page of my first book on the subject of preaching, *As One Without Authority* (1971), reads as follows:

To
My Mother
And
In Memory of
My Father
She taught me the Word
He taught me the words

Some of you may recognize in the inscription the two areas of study and teaching that were to occupy me all my adult life: Scripture and Preaching. And all who read this will already have guessed the source of my appreciation for stories and the model for my attempts at telling them. Once, following worship in my home church, a service at which I preached, an elderly parishioner said to me at the door, "You sound like your Daddy." I thanked him.

6

Three to a Bed

From the outset of this reflection on my early life, it has been
my hope that I would discover in an event or in a relationship,
or perhaps in some constellation of factors, pleasant or painful,
a hitherto unidentified key to my becoming a preacher. I have
tried to keep myself open and hospitable to such a discovery
without pressing too hard to locate and name such a moment.
There is nothing in me that insists that such a discovery be
made in order to validate my life as a preacher. I do believe that
the ways of God are not always obvious, and that an initiative of
God as important as calling a person to preach can be mediated,
and not necessarily be direct. The voice of God can sound very
much like that of a parent, or a sibling, or a friend, or even a
stranger. It is also a long-held conviction that while faith may
identify God at work in our lives, there must be available to one's
reason another way to explain what happened. Faith can be so
certain and confident that in reflection no other explanation
makes sense; still, faith must be a choice, not coerced, a "Yes"
when a "No" was available.

I say this at this point because I want you to know that it
has been my expectation to discover an important factor in my

call in remembering my relationships with my siblings. After all, it was with them that I spent so much of my early and formative years. It was with them that I ate, played, fought, and slept. If God had something special to say to me, they provided a ready and available voice. So far, however (and I say "so far" because I continue to remember as I write), I have been disappointed. This is not to speak negatively of them; by no means. They laughed and cried, played and worked, ate and slept, with no awareness of any possibility of being instruments of God in my life, just as I was unaware at the time of God having anything in mind for me.

My biggest disappointment in this recollection as it bears on my sister and my brothers is that their major impact on my memory was as a group, as the population of the house. This can be understood, as I will seek to explain, but my present concern is that you not think it impersonal and unfair, as though I thought of them as faceless and nameless, without individuation. Nothing could be farther from the truth. Before I attempt to explain in what way they impacted my life more as a group than as individuals, a sister and three brothers, let me briefly introduce them to you.

Frieda, my sister and the first born, was supposed to be a boy. So the midwife told my mother, and so the plan was to name the first-born son Fred, after my father. The name had to be modified to Frieda. And Frieda never tried to be a boy; nothing about her was tomboyish. I have no memory of her riding a mule, catching frogs, or wearing overalls. She clearly did not feel the need to compete with her brothers. Why should she? As the eldest, she was in charge in Momma's absence. "While I am gone, mind your sister; if you don't you will answer to me." Even though she was 100 percent girl, playing with dolls and dress up, Frieda had power. And she had Daddy wrapped around her finger. When our horse and wagon went to town, she sat up front beside Daddy; her brothers were piled in the back. When I began school she was already in the sixth grade, another world. She was quiet and self-conscious, but moved into the teen years with a flourish, making friends at school and in church. Her entrance into church life was natural and seamless, delighting in opportunities to lead and to serve. So it was all her life, loved by all, young and old. Were she born into a world and a church that regarded women differently, she might have been a minister. She loved her family and kept each one aware of and in contact with the others. She was gushingly proud of her preacher brother. Frieda "understood" Daddy better than the rest of us and let her love cover his multitude of sins. She married but was without children. Following Momma's debilitating stroke, Frieda took her into her own home and cared for her until Momma's death. A regret of my life is that I did not give more attention to my relation to Frieda. She was my older sister and seemingly self-sufficient, and so years passed before I realized that older sisters need younger brothers, and vice versa. But to this day it pleases me to be "Miss Frieda's brother."

Walter was four years my senior and for years my model. He was the most handsome of us and the tallest, finally ascending to the height of 5 feet, 10 inches! He was intelligent, articulate, athletic (he lettered in eight-man football at Lambuth College), and popular. He saw the humor in practically everything, able to keep Momma laughing even on the darkest days. And as I was later to realize, he was, even in childhood, a master at disguising his thoughts and feelings. Walter used his wit to get the best of his brothers. For example, when dividing a stick of peppermint between two of us, he would make the initial break, then nibble alternately one piece and then the other until his younger brothers, at first admiring how carefully he tried to be fair and then suddenly aware how much of our candy he was consuming, ran crying to Momma calling for Walter's execution. Or, for example, as in all things, we took turns riding the bicycle (a used bike, purchased by a prosperous cousin for five dollars). Always, after taking his turn, Walter had to "fix" something on the bike, after which he had to make a trial run to make sure it was "fixed." There was no end to his mastery over his brothers, but always with charm and good humor.

Walter took his turn becoming a member of the church, in his place on the pew with Momma. But even a sacred sanctuary did not dull the edge of his mischief. When a congregational hymn was announced, he turned quickly to the number, and by the time the singing began, he had composed other words, which he sang with gusto. Momma reprimanded him, of course, but we all could tell her heart was not fully in the reprimand. She seemed a bit proud of his ability. It was his hymn revising that first made me aware of his love of and skill with words. Walter moved more and more into the world of words. He wrote for school papers, then he worked part-time for the town newspaper, which often published his poems and articles. After his service in the Army Air Corps, he attended the School of Journalism of the University of Missouri. With advancements appropriate to his abilities, he became finally the publisher and editor of a newspaper. It was evident in his speaking and writing that he was proud of his preacher brother, with whom he exchanged stories. He was an excellent storyteller, but it was in more than storytelling that he was becoming Daddy. Tobacco and alcohol took more and more of his life until his death at forty-seven. What a tragic loss, still to this day.

Alvin is two years my senior and grows old quietly and alone, having lost last year his wife of fifty-nine years. Al is more like Momma's side of the family, both in appearance and in general disposition. In his growing up Al was very quiet, apparently believing you should talk only if you have something to say. And his shyness was extreme. If the family was at the table having a meal and someone knocked at the door, Al took his plate and retreated to the backyard until the visitor left. Eating for him was a private matter; no spectators allowed. In our childhood days, when Al talked it was primarily about what he imagined a bright future would be. Some day he would build a town, a new town, containing everything he did not presently have, but would possess someday. He would not work in that future world. He would own a large restaurant in which was prepared his favorite foods. The door would be locked, he being the only customer. Between the unhappy and deprived present and that happy future, Al seemed to me to be marking time. I think he was, in ways more painful than I realized in our growing up, a victim of the Depression. I do not speak only of the Depression, which engulfed the whole country, but also of the additional depression created by alcoholism in the home. To this day, Al asks, "How did we survive? How did we live through our childhood?" He does not ask seeking an answer; Al does not like to remember; he changes the subject.

Al never had any pretense about him; he used no skills of wit or words to make things appear better than they were. He lived for the time when he could move out of his unwanted present. And the way out for him was not education; he hated school. School was not only boring and uninteresting; it was embarrassing. School is competitive socially and Al (as were we all) was not playing on a level field. We were not only poor; we were noticeably poor. So Al's way out was time: "When I am old enough." As soon as he was of age he joined the Navy, where he served through World War II. He announced his departure from high school with a message on the blackboard:

> This is my motto
> As Admiral Farragut said,
> "Damn the torpedoes,
> Full speed ahead!"

Al left the Navy a new person. The old reticence, the social tardiness, the extreme shyness was gone. He stood on his own, free, eye-to-eye with anyone. He engages family, friends, and strangers alike. He travels and makes good company wherever he is. And strange as it may seem, Al also entered the world of words. For years he was the actual printer of a newspaper, and for years he formatted the *Journal of the American Medical Association*. And Al tells a pretty good story.

Roland, the youngest of the family, is four and one half years my junior. That fact alone tells you something of the disadvantages and the advantages of his life. With siblings four, six, eight, and ten years his senior, he was both spoiled and resented. He was "the baby," with all the privileges appertaining thereto. For a time I resented him. Until he came along, I was the youngest and, as such, enjoyed hearing Momma say, "Make a place for Bud" (Bud was my name at home); "Save some for Bud"; "Let Bud play": "Now it is Bud's turn." Now, all that privilege was gone; there was a new kid in the house. An advantage for Roland was the election in the year of his birth of Franklin D. Roosevelt as President of the United States. Change was in the air; soon the W.P.A., the C.C.C., and other programs of the National Recovery Act would begin to chase the gloom and gnawing poverty in America. Happy days were here again, but in Roland's early memories, his mother had a job, his sister worked after school, and his brothers sold newspapers. We had moved to town before Roland's third birthday, so he has no memory of the farm and the old home place. To this day he feels the absence of those memories and welcomes family gatherings at which there is a lot of remembering. Quite unlike Al, he wants to hear how it was. Visits to cemeteries and albums of old photographs are important to him.

I do not wish to be misunderstood: the move to the town was not a move from darkness to light, from poverty to plenty. On the contrary, the move was compulsory and a low point for the family. If town offered some opportunity for employment, meager and low-paying as it was, Daddy was unwilling or unable to take advantage of it. His drinking became more debilitating. Roland has few happy memories of his relation to Daddy. In fact, I imagine his memory is generally one of inattention and neglect. Momma doubled her efforts to be mother and father, but she had to go to work. And, of course, he still had a sister and three brothers who alternated between spoiling Roland and complaining about his tagging along.

Like the rest of us, Roland followed Momma to Sunday school and worship. And like Walter and Alvin, but unlike Brenning, Roland took his turn in the military. The war was over, but the G.I. Bill provided support for college and, as no small benefit, the opportunity to get away, to find one's place, to be on one's own.

Perhaps it comes as no surprise to the reader that Roland also entered the world of words. His major was communication and for a time he was a reporter for a Memphis newspaper. Apparently the starvation pay of a fledgling reporter was for Roland too much like the old days of his childhood and youth, and so he left the newspaper for the world of business. Yet there remains in him a story to be written. It may yet appear. When we visit we still pile up words on each other.

I said early in this particular essay that the major impact of my siblings on my memory is not as individuals but as a group, as the principal population in our home. I took time to introduce each of them in the hope that some memory might be triggered in the process. Perhaps one or more of my siblings might have contributed in some special way to my being called to preach. If there are dots there, you will have to help me connect them. My present concern is to attend to the impact of being one of five on my vocational journey.

I hope my parents and my siblings will forgive me for seeming to be unfeeling, but in my early years I had the uncomfortable feeling of being crowded; there were, it seemed, too many people in the house. I cannot speak for all boys, but from the early years until the present I have a strong need for periods of privacy. Three boys in one bed was not only a fact, but also a symbol of my childhood. I was not being abused, of course not. The house was too small for seven occupants, and really too small when Momma, with her wonderful Christian hospitality, welcomed others who were orphaned or no longer welcome in their own families. My need for time alone was often a need unmet. Ordinarily one's bed is a place of refuge, but not if it is already occupied. There were places to go and I made use of them: the hayloft, the smokehouse, under the back porch.

I trust my memory when I say that I did not retreat to feel sorry for myself, to wish I were someone else, or to blame my parents for not providing a larger house. From this distance it seems I was not worrying my parents' worries, even though I do recall overhearing them in private conversations about our illnesses, the lack of money, and other topics that occupy parents. I think my need for space, for privacy, for time alone was not unhealthy nor unnatural. Probably all children need time alone to process events and relationships, to assimilate life, to interpret the why of things rather than always looking to others for clarity and understanding.

What was going on with me and in me was the development of my interior world; perhaps my interior world was larger than average. Maybe the lack of exterior space drove me to the most available space: my self. Certainly several circumstances conspired to move me inward. There was the sheer fact of isolation, living on a small farm miles from the nearest town and without transportation. That alone activates imagination. Then there were the illnesses—not only the usual childhood diseases, which brought the county health officer to post quarantine signs on our house, but the more serious ones such as malaria. I alone in the family contracted malaria. My strongest memories of that sickness are not so much of pain but of being removed from social exchange, even from my siblings, and of missing out on everything. Daddy pressed me into reading during this period, and I was somewhat successful in exchanging one world for another.

Whatever the causes, whatever the reasons, whatever the gains and losses, I am continually grateful for a large interior world, a world in which I could, when necessary, live alone quite comfortably, a world in which I could imagine, a world in which I could wonder and ponder, a world in which I eventually encountered God with age-appropriate questions, being alternately disturbed and comforted. Gradually God became for me "the Place."

7

School Days

I cannot say at this point whether or not I will find in early school days influences positive or negative on the call to preach. I cannot say because writing down certain memories often awakens other memories. I can say, however, that several attitudes and notions formed under the influence of public school had to be discarded later, or radically modified, before I could preach beyond prejudices and skewed social opinions. If you discern already that elementary school was not for me time happily spent, then you are right. I will not try to distinguish between perception and reality; when reflecting on formative forces in one's life, the perception *is* the reality. I do want to alert you to the fact that my life in grades one through six and grades seven through twelve was so different that I seem to be two different people, or school seems two different worlds. For this reason, it seems wise to separate these memories of school days into two essays.

Wild animals, especially the hunted ones, are able to survive not solely by keen eye and sensitive nose, but also by their invisibility. We do not know they are there; they seem absent even when present, even close at hand. Seeming to be absent, that was my strategy for survival. Going a full day without having my name called was a day ideal but not frequent enough. This is not to say that I was unprepared in my lessons. On the contrary, I was conscientious as a student and always received good marks from my teachers. I learned quite early that the unprepared students received more attention, and attention was definitely not what I wanted. To be honest, I enjoyed the reading, writing, and arithmetic; it was sharing with teachers and classmates what I had learned that was painful. That I was a good student was no proof of high intelligence; I had gotten a head start at home. Momma had made a family game of playing with words, mostly unusual words. We were to pronounce the word correctly, divide it into syllables, spell it, and use it in a sentence. Before entering first grade I could handle *disestablishmentarianism, correspondence, asafetida,* and all such words, which are the heart and soul of daily conversation among grade schoolers! And probably for a year before entering first grade, I sat at the homework table with Frieda, Walter, and Alvin. (Roland was too young.) After supper, Momma set the extra kerosene lamp in the center of an old library table. After false claims of not having any homework, a little pushing and shoving, and, "You're taking too much room," work began. I watched and listened and when a discarded piece of paper was available, I did my own homework. My questions were not treated with respect. "Why don't we say 'two mouses'? We say 'two houses.'" "What letter comes after Z?" "Do you want to hear me count?" By the time I entered first grade I had answers to questions the teachers never asked. Thank goodness!

In case you haven't guessed, I was very undersocialized and I was thrown suddenly into a competitive environment. The boys and girls who lived in town seemed already to know each other and the teacher seemed to take that to mean we all knew each other. Wrong; I knew no one. On the first day, the teacher said we would begin by telling where we went on vacation last summer. Vacation? What's a vacation? Stories of Washington, D.C.; Miami; Smoky Mountains; and New Orleans had me drawn in a knot. "We're out of time; we'll finish tomorrow." Thank goodness. That night I asked Daddy what I could say. "Son, she is your teacher; do what she says. She is asking you for a lie, so tell her one." I did. My family had gone to all the places already mentioned plus a few extra. The teacher took me out of the room. She asked why I lied, and I blubbered out that I didn't want to be laughed at. When we returned to the room, there were no more vacation reports. The other poor children were spared.

The same feeling of embarrassment arose again in me when the teacher announced the lunchroom procedure. At ten minutes before noon, a bell would ring. All children getting free lunches would stand beside their desks and march to the cafeteria. At five minutes after noon, a second bell would ring, at which sound those paying for their lunches would stand beside their desks and march to the cafeteria. I don't think the teacher or the principal had any clue about a child's feeling, marching as charity children in front of their classmates. A sign around the neck would announce even more clearly, "We are the poor." I did not march; I lied about having brought a lunch. I never ate a free lunch. There are things worse than being hungry. Too proud? Maybe. Too sensitive? Maybe. Momma and Daddy never knew. Momma would have said, "It is no disgrace to be poor." Daddy would have said, "Tell them what they can do with their free lunch." Neither did they know that I never wore at school the sweater brought to our house along with other used clothing. The sweater fit my body but not my self-esteem. I removed it on the way to school and hid it under the Sugar Creek bridge. I put it on again on my way home. I congratulated myself that the boy who wore it when it was new never had the opportunity to identify it on the school playground.

Call me greedy, but the memory of having something new, something that never belonged first to anyone else, is still a bright memory for me. After a strong storm of wind and rain, I went outside to play. On the ground in front of me was a one-dollar bill. I rushed inside to tell my mother, all the while staking claim to it. As I predicted, she said we must return it to its owner. She sent word of the find to the neighbors while I continued to call off the search. Finally, she said it was mine. Visions of sugarplums! But Momma had other plans. We went to town and with one dollar she bought for me a pair of bibbed overalls with matching shirt. The overalls had pockets in front, pockets on the sides, pockets in back, and pockets in the bib. As soon as we were home, I filled the pockets: marbles, small knife, magnet, magnifying glass, and the foot of a chicken that would send the girls screaming away. I paraded to school on Monday. In fact, sometimes I would sit on the porch just to watch myself go by.

My worst class? Health. The questions were tough: Do you sleep near an open window? Do you drink three glasses of milk every day? Do you eat two pieces of fruit every day? Do you eat three green leafy vegetables every day? Who could pass such a class? But the worst part was the coming of the County Health Nurse to examine us. She checked ears, necks, hands, fingernails, and teeth. I flunked teeth; a dentist was out of the question. And she checked our hair for lice. I passed lice, but I was angered that she carefully scratched through the hair of six or eight boys, including me, but hardly paused to glance at the heads of the others. All who passed the physical and gave the right answer to the questions were given Blue Ribbons, ceremoniously, with a nice certificate, with smiles of approval. Then, on the appointed day, the Blue Ribbon pupils marched behind a full band down Main Street to rounds of applause. The less than healthy ones were sent into a classroom to do homework under the watchful eye of a supervising teacher. I found a Blue Ribbon on the playground and wore it home, hoping to prove to my mother how healthy I was, but she knew better.

My worst day in school? Valentine's Day, no question. You remember the routine, I'm sure. The teacher brings to class a beautifully decorated box with a slot in the top through which the boys and girls insert their valentines. Near the close of the school day, the lid of the box is removed and one class member delivers the cards to the persons whose names are on them. After a few minutes, the rough-edged boys who have not gotten a card yet begin to pretend they are glad not to be involved in all that "sissy stuff." The prettiest girl in class has a pile of cards; probably a million. The previous year I neither gave nor received a valentine. This year I gave one. I had no money to buy one, so I made a valentine out of tablet paper and put on it the name of the girl in class who befriended everyone the same. I wanted to see her reaction to my quite awful but sincere card. She opened it and smiled her thanks across the room. (At our sixtieth class reunion she told me she still had it.) Again, I received no card, while two or three harvested a lap full. The next year I received a card from the teacher. I was elated but then depressed upon seeing that every pupil in the class received one from her, and all her valentines were the same. Thoughtful and fair, but a bit too democratic for me. It failed to remove the sadness and loneliness of Valentine's Day. "Them that has, gets" was still true. But thank goodness, Valentine's Day with its terrible box ended that year, probably banned in all civilized societies as a relic of the time of class and privilege.

It was becoming clear to me that reading, writing, and arithmetic were only a fraction of what school was about. There were programs, traditions, and activities that perpetuated distinctions social and economic, having nothing to do with classroom performance. Had I been from a family that gave little or no emotional support, no positive reinforcement, I very likely would have been a drop out somewhere along the way. Making good grades alone will not sustain a child's spirit; sooner or later there must be a sense of belonging, a sense of being welcomed into a circle of peers.

Before I moved out of grade school into junior high (middle school) I made one last effort to receive my place in the affection and respect of my classmates. In my school there were not different teachers for different subjects; the teacher in whose class you were placed taught all the subjects. In the segment called "Science," the teacher burned considerable energy trying to get us excited about the telegraph, how it worked and how it moved civilization rapidly forward. She even brought a telegraph key to class; we learned the Morse code and in class tapped out single and simple words. It was in this extended segment on the telegraph that two tragedies occurred, both social, and both all the more tragic because they stemmed from the intent to yield social dividends to this undersocialized boy. Tragedy number one: the teacher tells us about the inventor, Samuel F. B. Morse. A classmate, pretending an appetite for more knowledge, asks, "What does the F. B. stand for?" The teacher doesn't know. She asks the class; no one knows—except for me. Now is my chance to stand tall in the esteem of both the class and the teacher. She acknowledges my raised hand. "F. B. stands for Fred Brenning." (His real name was Samuel Finley Breese Morse.) "Brenning, how did you know that? Were you named for him?" "Yes, ma'am." The spotlight was on me. Named for a famous scientist, and in this very room; I am racking up points fast! The only thing dulling the aura was the fact that I lied, and with a mother like mine you never lied well. I don't know what I told myself to wipe the lie off my face. Maybe it was a child's version of a temporary suspension of the ethical in the service of my pitiful ego. Nice try, but it didn't work; Momma had put a keen edge on my conscience. In the lunch hour I went to the teacher and told the truth. She asked why I did it, and I told the truth: I wanted to impress my classmates. She commended me for coming forward and assigned my punishment. I was to tell the class, which I did. Some snickered, some were disappointed, and some said they never believed it anyway. So much for my effort to improve my lot socially: one small step up, one giant step down. How could things be any worse? I was soon to find out.

Tragedy number two: the exercise using the telegraph key continued the next day. I was called on first to tap out a word, and the class was to identify the word. Still shaken and embarrassed from tragedy number one, I could remember none of the Morse code. I froze, but hoping none of the class would remember either, I tapped out a few letters at random. Before the teacher could ask the class for my chosen word, a bright girl blurted out, "Uh oh, Brenning said an ugly word!" The giggles turned to laughter, I was taken to the principal's office, put in after-school detention for a week. And in social purgatory for eternity. I was generally shunned except for the ruffians in the class who applauded my efforts. They did not believe me when I explained that I did not know I had tapped out an ugly word. What that word was, I do not know to this day.

I need to go no further with sad stories in order for you to understand my failure to open doors through which I could walk into a modicum of popularity. The doors into a new and different social world are often more difficult to open than was the heavy door into the boys' restroom in that elementary school. My first few efforts with that door failed as well; I was too small, it was too big. Soon I learned to stand and wait until a bigger boy came alone. When he opened the door I slipped in behind him. Those bigger boys never knew what a gift of relief they gave me. And where was Alvin, my brother two years older and stronger? He was never there when I needed him. As far as I know, he never went to the restroom during his six years in that building.

And so my early school years were spent alternating between hiding in my large interior world and trying to make a place for myself with efforts that were counterproductive due primarily to my hiding from the very people whose acceptance I wanted. I had no social strategy as a child, of course, but from this distance I can see what I was doing. For example, I would want to invite a classmate to come out to our little farm to play. Then I would tell myself that he would probably not want to come. Therefore, rather than be hurt by his rejection, I would not invite him. In other words, protecting my feelings was regularly my posture even when it was neither reasonable nor successful. I am sure I was not alone in such social dysfunction. Even some adults are trapped in the same place.

Now I wish to move to my experience of school, grades seven through twelve. The memories now to be reported are of a very different nature. The differences that you will clearly observe were, in part, due to changes in me, but others were the results of my responses to events that I did not initiate. And I must at this point project ahead to my becoming a part of an institution—or, better, a community—alongside school, which affected me strongly, both in and out of school. I refer to the church.

8

School Days

(Continued)

You can imagine with what pleasure I turn away from my early fumbling to discover, to develop, to be a self in my first social context beyond family. Whether or not the pains of those efforts were peculiar to me, I do not know. Neither do I know in what ways, if any, those classroom and playground experiences were venues for the voice of God. That memories of those days remain vivid persuade me that they were formative, evidence of which remains in the warp and woof of my life. I feel no need to identify more specifically those influences, nor will I enter into evaluating them, nor do I have plans to seek out an exorcist. I learned long ago that in turning one's life over to God even dark threads can be woven into a pattern that could not be anticipated then, nor fully understood even now.

So now we turn away from elementary school days to enter into the enjoyable events and relationships of junior high and high school. I will, however, pause to relate one encounter that actually occurred near the end of my sixth grade, but had positive effects for my future in school. I do not say the results were positive in an attempt to justify what was in itself a regrettable incident. It was an act of violence and my mother had persuaded me, over my father's objection, that an act of violence cannot be justified. The occasion was the annual Strawberry Festival in our town and I was watching the parade down Main Street from the vantage point of the high bank in front of the elementary school. Suddenly and shockingly I felt a strong push against my back and I went tumbling down the bank to the edge of the street. I had been pushed by one of the bullies (we had an abundance) in my class. It was not an act of getting even with me; we hardly had any contact. His attack was unprovoked. I climbed back up and told him what he already knew: he had no cause to do that, I had done nothing to him, and that I could have really been hurt had I fallen into the street. With that I resumed my place, watching the parade. I assumed it was over. It was not. Again, I went tumbling down the hill to the street curb. Again, I climbed back up the bank, but this time I hit him with my left fist, knocking him to the ground, his mouth and nose bleeding. "Now look what you've done!" he said as he ran away. My thumb was bleeding, and I had lost interest in the parade. I went home—trembling, of course, not only because I am not a fighter and I had fought, but also because I had to face Momma. It was a very emotional time, the upshot of which was that Momma apologized to his mother and I apologized to him. He never bothered me again. Was it my left fist or the apology that ended it? Momma said it was the apology. We all know what Daddy would say.

As I remember it, this was my only fight, assuming the usual scuffles with brothers do not count. I did come close one other time. I have told you of Nicey Rounds, midwife at our births; of Robert, her son, in prison for a crime he did not commit; and of his son Robert Jr., my age. The Rounds family withdrew from whites, and our loss of the farm and move to town further separated us. When we were entering our teens Robert Jr. and I met on the street. He was angry, hostile, full of threats and hate toward all whites. This was a different Robert

Jr. "I can understand your anger, but not toward me," I said. "You're white, aren't you?" He moved closer, he pushed, he badmouthed me, but I was confident he did not really want to hurt me. He could have; he was much larger. He began to cry, and so did I. He ran down the railroad tracks, probably much the same way he did about a year later. Trying to catch a freight train to visit his father, Robert Jr. slipped and fell beneath the train. His leg was severed and he bled to death. I miss him.

Now you know all about my fighting. What you have yet to know is the response of classmates to my fight on parade day. None of them were present to see it, but news of it, slightly exaggerated, was all over the school. I was not so much a hero as I was a surprise. The smallest boy in class conquers the school bully! David and Goliath all over again! I confess, I made no effort to correct the exaggerated versions of the fight. The benefits were many: students who did not know me now greeted me by name. I no longer was the last one chosen in pick up baseball and football games. My classroom performance was no longer the achievement of a geek; I was a normal person. My name appeared in nominations for class offices. Signs of greater acceptance appeared every day. I was having my fifteen minutes of fame, but in this case, the fifteen minutes stretched into six years of public school.

Before I continue this recital of my happier days, I need to pause to ask if my fight with the bully was really at the heart of my life's turnaround. In many ways, I hope all this difference in my social life did not hinge on the fight. I hope not, because I am not a fighter and did not wish to harvest benefits from an act of violence. While I enjoyed the social gains, I secretly hoped that the fight was not cause but coincidence. And, actually, to say my classmates gave me positive marks because I hit another classmate would be an insult to them. My classmates were in the main of such character as to set little premium on fighting. In fact, I want to turn our attention to the extraordinary quality of that class. I genuinely think that the fight gave me some attention, but there were other and more important factors that sustained my continuing to receive positive regard and to begin building life friendships.

First, we need to remember that the country was coming out of the Great Depression, which was not only an economic but also an emotional and mental condition. Some families experienced depression in all the meanings of that word. Ours was one such family. The oft-repeated, "But some families are hurting more than we are," did not cheer up any of us. I still hate some of the old sayings passed along as helpful and encouraging. For example, "I had no shoes and was sad until I met a man with no feet." Plenty of cheer for everyone there. But the country was now experiencing better days, and so was the Craddock family.

Second, when I was in junior high school, we moved out of the small house on a dirt street without electricity or plumbing. Except for Daddy and the youngest, Roland, every member of the family contributed to the family income. The house to which we moved was on a gravel street, had electricity, plumbing, and natural gas. Out with the woodstove, in with gas heaters and a gas cook stove; out with kerosene lamps, in with electric lights; out with the outhouse, in with the restroom. Within two years a do-it-yourself shower was added to the sink and stool. And did I mention a telephone? On a party line, but a telephone. I will not continue this recital; I just want the reader to know (or remember) what these changes meant to the socialization of a small, shy, self-absorbed, often embarrassed boy. I do not mean to imply that I was economically determined, but it does make a difference whose clothes you are wearing. Frieda was beginning to date and the boys could now call for her at home rather than simply meeting her at the restaurant or theater.

Finally, skills and abilities I had used to disguise fears, embarrassment, and low self-esteem now were freed to serve the common good and to contribute to the health of the groups to which I belonged. I do not think it is merely boasting when I say that I was a contributing factor in the creation of what became a most extraordinary class at Humboldt High School.

For example, I had used humor both as a shield and as a weapon in my earlier extremely self-conscious days. Now others enjoyed my humor and found it helpful in liberating their own. Humor free of barbs is community-creating. Seeing the humor in life, even in different or demanding situations, was not consciously developed; it was a gift from both parents. Daddy found in everything an interesting story; Momma could heal pain with a little song created on the spot. My love of words, again a gift from hearth and home, had earlier been used to talk my way out of discomfort or embarrassment; now I was sometimes called on to speak for and to speak to my peers. I began to write articles for the school paper. Before I finished high school, I served as president of the student body and gave the valedictory address at commencement. And even my athletic abilities, meager as they were, came to be appreciated. I had the speed to compete in the 100-yard dash, and in spite of my small frame, I played quarterback on our football team without embarrassing the team or myself (it was a small school). I felt good to be a member of the team, rather than school mascot or some such diminishing role.

I became so bold and free that in my senior year I made a few efforts at dating, but not without setbacks. My pattern had been to entertain the possibility of perhaps maybe considering asking an attractive classmate to a school party, and then upon further thought, telling myself she probably already had a date, so I went alone. Later I would punish myself with regret. My social life was essentially regret. But in my senior year, emboldened by a football victory or election to a class office, I had the nerve to actually ask, and several girls said yes. But dating was not a big deal, no measure of popularity, no social statement; many of us were good friends, went together to parties and dances, and had a good time.

I have spoken of my high school class as extraordinary, and it was. I have not researched it, but I daresay the grade point average for the class was well above average. The percentage of the Class of 1946 to go on to college and to have professional careers was unusually high, and among those who could not or chose not to continue their education, many made excellent contributions to family, church, and community. And not least among the credits of this class has been our pleasure in each other's company. We delight in reunions, of which there have been many. Along the way we had some good teachers, but I think a major impetus to excellence in the class was the fact that we brought out the best in each other. And while there were cases to the contrary, by and large, friendships and mutual respect were not impeded by differences in social or economic status among the families of class members. In my elementary school days I judged fellow pupils from a distance and concluded that those from prosperous and respected families thought they were superior. As I came to know them later, it was clear I was wrong. I rained on my own parade, imagining rejection when acceptance was there for the taking. I recall once having a blind date in a nearby town, a date secured for me (as part of a double-date) by a classmate with a car. When we drove up to my date's house, I thought, "Wow! What a mansion!" I looked at myself—blue jeans, knit shirt, and unimpressive frame— and urged my friend, unsuccessfully, to back out and speed away. Cautiously, I rang the doorbell. A butler answered. "And whom shall I say is calling?" I finally thought of my name, out she came, we introduced ourselves, and off we went, the four of us, to a delightful evening. No haves and have-nots here. Thank God I gradually lost the common prejudice of the poor against the prosperous.

I have been talking to you about high school days, and now it is time to introduce the subject of vocation. Now that I was graduating, what next? Of course, I gave serious thought to my future, but the focus of that thinking was not directly in response to any event or relationship at school. By this time in my life, church was a vital and formative influence, and to that influence we turn next. However, the teacher at school who served as vocational counselor to me was aware of my growing interest in some form of church service or Christian ministry.

We talked several times at length. I seldom spoke to anyone else of this orientation toward ministry. I was not sure and did not know how to become sure. She was sensitive and caring.

After several conversations, my counselor (whether or not she was really a counselor, I do not know) began to offer options: "There are many ways to minister." "There are many ministers who are not in the pulpit." "There are some very valuable and satisfying ministries without pulpits." Soon it was obvious she was steering me away from preaching. Why? She said she hated to see me hurt or disappointed, that I should think realistically. She talked about the size of the pulpit and of my size. She said most churches would not have public address systems and that my voice was soft and did not carry well. Since there were so many other forms of Christian ministry, why not avoid hindrances that surely would come between me and the pulpit? She made sense, a great deal of sense. The conversation was discouraging. I did not react with, "I'll show them"; I pondered her advice, but I did not give up on preaching. I did wonder, however, why it seemed that God wanted me not only to be a minister but to be a preacher. Was I being called to preach?

I ask the reader now to go with me to church. We will attend Sunday school, worship, and church camp.

9

Sunday School

I am a product of the Sunday school of Central Avenue Christian Church in Humboldt, Tennessee. I do not say this to fault the worship services or the preaching; the contributions of those two programs will be presented in the next essay. I simply wish to recognize that it was in Sunday school that I first experienced Christian community, that I first encountered adults outside my family who loved and encouraged me, and that I first was led through the Bible in a connected and almost narrative way. The move from the small family farm, lost to the bank during the Great Depression, was painful in many ways: a move from the familiar to the unfamiliar, a move from poverty amid poverty to poverty amid relative prosperity, a move from a noncompetitive to a competitive society. But the pain was not only made bearable but at times forgotten because of my experiences of church, and of Sunday school especially. I am glad we moved.

To those whose experience of Sunday school was or is less than memorable, I should say a word lest you think I am looking at a meaningless program through eyes misty with sentimentality. Nowadays it is not uncommon to visit churches with hundreds in worship and seventy in Sunday school, and many of that seventy lounging around the coffee or pop machines or shooting hoops in the church gym. Granted, many churches provide excellent educational experiences other than Sunday school, and some educators argue that Sunday school has outlived its usefulness. I am not entering that debate nor am I seeking to revive what once was. I only want the reader to know that there was a time and place when and where lives were deeply affected by Sunday school. I was in that time and place. At Central Avenue, attendance at Sunday school far exceeded attendance at worship. Attendance records were kept, absentees were contacted, superintendents presided over teacher's meetings, educational resources were distributed, visitors were recognized and welcomed, offerings were taken for missions of the church, prayers were learned and said, birthdays were noted, cards were signed and mailed to the sick and grieving, songs were sung, and reports on the state of the school were made periodically to the official board of the church. And Sunday school classes provided the structure for social events.

At Central Avenue the classes for children were held on the ground floor of a large brick building. Access to the upper floor was by stairs inside and concrete steps outside. To a small boy from the farm, it was an impressive building, saying to all who entered, "Behave yourself and be reverent."

According to the Sunday school records, I had been enrolled in the Cradle Roll, not because I was present, but because my parents were members of the church. There were no "privileges or responsibilities appertaining thereto"; they simply kept records and knew that I existed. My memory of Sunday school begins in the Primary Department: school grades one, two, and three. And first among those memories is the welcome I received. Even though our clothing reflected a difference in the economic condition of the families of the pupils, I noted no such difference in the welcome, as highly sensitive as I was to such matters. Even when I learned that the charity shoes I was wearing were, in fact, girl's shoes, I found no reason to try to hide my feet. In the Primary Department there was "neither Jew nor Gentile." The chairs in which we sat were bright with many colors, and even brighter were the smiles of Miss Anna Sue and Miss Lucille, the two young women who played the piano and taught us to sing "Jesus loves me, this I know, for the Bible tells me so," and, "Jesus loves the little children of the world, red and yellow, black and white, they are precious in his sight, Jesus loves the little children of the world." It was years before I realized how revolutionary those songs were, clashing with the world in which I played and went to school. I do not know when I learned that Central Avenue was full of Craddocks, including Miss Ana Sue and Miss Lucille. Mr. Ben, a patriarch of the church, was their father and father to a houseful—all my cousins since he was my great uncle. But it was not a cousin's welcome that they gave me; rather it was a church welcome, the same as they gave everyone in the department. You can't imagine how much at home I felt.

The classroom was filled with pictures of Jesus and of other characters in the Bible. I thought they were actual photographs of Jesus holding children on his lap. Jesus walking on water, Jesus stilling a storm, Jesus feeding the hungry, Jesus healing the sick, Jesus teaching the people. Of course, there were pictures of Samson and Noah and David and Mary and John the Baptist and Paul, but Jesus outnumbered them all. These characters came to life in the stories the teachers told, but Jesus outshone them all. I was becoming attached to Jesus in ways I did not understand at the time.

It was a sad day when Miss Jane told us she was getting married and moving away. She was moving to Mississippi and her name would no longer be Jane Nelson but Jane Manning. Becoming mother to Archie and grandmother to Peyton and Eli came too late to ease our pain at her leaving. You see, Miss Jane helped relieve the boredom of having to stay for church following Sunday school. She gave to our mother leaflets containing dots and numbers. While the preacher sawed the air and filled the sanctuary with "ought," "must," and "should," Miss Jane's pupils were busy connecting the dots: changing puzzles into pictures of Noah's ark; the Jerusalem temple; a returning prodigal; and, of course, Jesus teaching, feeding, and healing. I think I was in the Junior Department before I looked up and paid attention to the preacher.

It was in the Junior Department (school grades four, five, and six) that I came under the influence of Miss Emma Sloan. If I remember correctly, except for occasional substitutes, Miss Emma was my teacher for all three years. Was it her choice to remain with us, or was no one else willing to take us on? I don't know. I do know that she was a no-nonsense teacher who expected us to "be still and know that I am God." She read lengthy passages from the Bible with very few interpretive comments. Let me isolate three events from those three years, which may impress on the reader something of her impact on my life. Please be aware of something Miss Emma realized, which I did not: we in that class were approaching the age at which it was customary to make a confession of faith and receive baptism, becoming accountable members of the church. As I look back on it, I am persuaded Miss Emma was aware every Sunday of her responsibility to lead us into that sobering transition.

First, Miss Emma gave me my first Bible. Actually, it was a New Testament and Psalms, *King James Version*. Inside it she signed it, "Your teacher, Miss Emma Sloan." Beneath her signature she wrote, "May this book be a lamp for your feet and a light for your pathway." She urged the class to read the Bible every evening and to bring it with us to class every Sunday. Her opinion of the Old Testament, I do not know; the New Testament and Psalms was her textbook, and of that I would guess 75 percent of her lessons were on the gospels. In other words, she talked to us about Jesus. But the overarching and unforgettable truth was that I had a Bible, my very own Bible, and I began in a new way to read the Bible—perhaps, if I may say so, as though it was written for me.

Second, it was in Miss Emma's class that I asked my first questions, at least, the first I can recall. It was Christmastime and now that we all had Bibles, Miss Emma had us read around the room until we completed Luke's account of the birth of Jesus. For some reason, Miss Emma chose to give an economic interpretation of the story. Mary and Joseph were away from home and poor and could not afford a room at an inn. She described the stable and explained what a manger was. At that point she went ahead in the story to the dedication of the baby. At a dedication, she explained, parents were to make an offering of a lamb, but if you were poor, you were allowed to give two doves. Mary and Joseph gave two doves. The whole class was emotionally in Mary's and Joseph's corner; that is, until I asked my question. "If Mary and Joseph were so poor, what did they do with all that gold, frankincense, and myrrh that the wise men brought?" I wasn't trying to be a smart mouth or play "stump the teacher"; I was seeking information. Miss Emma looked at me sternly and said, "We're not supposed to question the Bible." After worship that day, she told my mother that I had raised a question about the Bible. On the way home Momma told me not to disturb the class by asking questions. "Just be quiet and listen," she said. And I did. I had other questions, but I kept them to myself.

Third, and most importantly, Miss Emma taught me how to carry the Bible in my head and heart so that I would have it when I needed it. "Sometimes," she said, "there may not be a Bible handy." Whether original with her or not, I don't know, but she gave to the class verses from the Bible according to letters of the alphabet (we were allowed to skip "x" and "z"), and urged us to memorize them. She had us say them in class, but since several students were irregular in attendance and uninterested in the assignment, finding it too much like school, Miss Emma finally abandoned the project. But I always found memorizing easy, and even fun, sometimes discovering I had "learned by heart" a poem or a famous speech when not even intending to do so. Thus it was that I carried in my mind and heart

twenty-four verses of the Bible and I still do to this day, just as
Miss Emma taught me when I was eleven years old.

A A soft answer turns away wrath.
B Be ye kind one to another, tender hearted, forgiving each
       other.
C Come unto me all you who labor and are heavy laden and
       I will give you rest.
D Do unto others as you would have them do unto you.
E Every good and perfect gift comes down from above.
F For God so loved the world that He gave His only begotten
       son.
G God is love.
H Have this mind in you which was in Christ Jesus.
I I am the way, the truth, and the life.
J Jesus Christ is the same yesterday, today, and forever.
K Know ye that the Lord is God.
L Love one another.
M Many are called but few are chosen.
N No one comes to the Father but by me.
O Open wide your hearts to receive us.
P Pray without ceasing.
Q Quicken my spirit according to your loving kindness.
R Repent and turn again.
S Speak the truth in love.
T The Word of God abides forever.
U Upon this rock I will build my church and the gates of hell
       will not prevail against it.
V Verily, verily, I say unto you, I am the door for the sheep.
W Whosoever will may come.
Y You shall love the Lord your God with all your heart and
       mind and soul and strength.

Thousands of times, in situations of joy or sorrow, alone
or among strangers, disturbed or at peace, in my own bed
or beside the bed of another, standing or sitting, walking or
driving or flying, I have said these verses in my mind. On

two occasions especially I remember saying them aloud even though I was alone: the evening of my baptism and the evening of my ordination. Now and then I have thought that I might exchange some of these verses for others more relevant to my life. But I have always dropped the idea, for reasons as clear to you as to me.

I was surprised to learn how scarce and fragmentary are my memories of Sunday school during my teenage years, school grades seven through twelve. A few reasons suggest themselves. For instance, I do recall how brief the tenures of most of the teachers were, with some of them even filling in for someone who was herself or himself a fill in. Those in class could assume lack of continuity and lack of preparation among our teachers. Sometimes *no one* appeared, leaving us to talk of sports and school events. Apparently, few adults wanted to teach adolescents. For reasons not clear to me, the church attention on youth shifted from Sunday school to Sunday evening activities. At Sunday evening gatherings, called Christian Youth Fellowship, there was fun, fellowship, study, food, and frequent opportunities to join with other youth groups in nearby towns. Regularly these evening meetings opened with a time of worship and closed with singing in a Friendship Circle. I was impressed.

I must acknowledge also that a cause for my spotty memories of those years in Sunday school was my own poor attendance record. Most of my absences occurred within one calendar year. I had an after school and Saturday job at a small grocery, which remained open until 11:00 p.m. on Saturday. I was tired and slept late on Sunday mornings in spite of Momma's repeated efforts to stir me. I thought she would finally give up; she never did. Usually I got up in time for worship at eleven, avoiding if I could Momma's eyes. My excuses were wasted on her, and frankly, on me as well. While it appeared my interest in church had waned, the fact is, the opposite was true. Let me explain.

In our church it was customary on Easter Sunday for twelve and thirteen year olds to make confessions of faith and to receive Christian baptism, either Easter evening or the following Sunday. Baptism was by immersion. When I was twelve I was in the group instructed by the pastor on the meanings of confession of faith and baptism. All in the group responded favorably on Easter morning, except for me. I was present but remained seated with my mother, to whom I later explained that I was not quite ready. I explained to myself that I did not wish simply to join the group. Some of them struck me as unready and nonserious, giggling nervously. I was overly serious, heavy with the thought of giving my life to God. I carried the weight of that commitment a full year, and at age thirteen, but not on Easter, I went before the congregation and made my confession of faith. My baptism did not occur for another three weeks, during which time I had my fourteenth birthday. The minister, Jack McCullough, was still in his theological studies at Vanderbilt, and for some reason was not immediately available for my baptism. In preparation, I fasted one day, recited several times the memory verses learned under Miss Emma Sloan, prayed, and wondered. Will baptism make me feel different? Do I talk about it to anyone? How will my life change? What do I do next? Completely in earnest I gave my life to God; I felt afraid and exhilarated, and I knew I did not want to lose the meaning of my baptism. My seriousness was general and without focus. I needed direction but found none. I kept my feelings to myself but found myself blaming others for their lack of interest in my spiritual welfare. Rather than carry my burdens alone I found it easier to unload them. This I did, in part, by absenting myself more frequently from Sunday school and God. Interest in my spiritual life did not wane in me; I simply was of the opinion that I could make it wane, and therefore, give myself relief from what was really going on. In retrospect it is clear that I interpreted my baptism as my ordination to ministry. But I was fourteen years old.

I spoke earlier of a lack of committed Sunday school teachers during these years. I wish now to modify that statement by mentioning two extraordinary persons whose brief time with me had lasting influence. Carl Wade Humphreys was my Sunday school teacher for less than one year. He was my only male teacher. Female teachers were so much the norm that I wondered why a man would be our teacher. Besides that, World War II had begun and young men in the church were leaving weekly for military service. "Why is Carl Wade still here?" I wondered. Before long the character of the man dissolved my question. He was kind, patient with the foolish, took our questions seriously, and manifested a passion about the Christian faith without appearing religious. He could laugh and cry with integrity. He treated each of us as individuals, but played no favorites. He was not a healthy man, but never made excuses and had no limp, emotional or physical. I admired and respected him immensely.

Mignonne Williams was never my Sunday school teacher; she was for a time the youth leader for our Sunday evening gatherings. She and her sister, Musedora, were, as their names indicate, different from others their age, but in indefinable ways. I never saw either of them in casual and carefree moods, yet they were kind, attentive to others, pleasant, and approachable. Their father was our family physician. Musedora, the older sister, I barely knew, but Mignonne was an important presence in my life. There was a formal and disciplined quality about her, always neat, well-dressed, prepared, and the leader without having to show it or prove it. She was not the hayride and hot dog type. She was elegant but not arrogant, attentive without needing attention, shy but not self-absorbed. She was our teacher, our advisor, and our friend. Relating to her was an experience of intimate distance. There was no one else like her in my life in those days. Whether school or work took her away, I do not know, but I, and we, missed her. I missed her answers to my questions, her stability and always being present, her patience with a boy who was serious about God but who tried to conceal it. And I missed the mystery about her; when she was giving of herself to us, you were very aware there was much more to her than anyone knew. Everyone should have a least one such person in his or her life.

10

Staying for Church

Worship at Central Avenue Christian Church during my boyhood was referred to as "church," as in the question, "Momma, do I have to stay for church?" Worship occurred twice on Sunday, in the morning following Sunday school, in the evening following Christian Youth Fellowship. Stated this way, the reader can see my priorities, Sunday school and CYF. There was a mid-week service on Wednesday evening, referred to as "Prayer Meeting," consisting of Bible study and prayers by the attendees. I seldom attended on Wednesday evening; those present were few and mostly older people. I did attend during the brief tenure of a pastor named Foster, for reasons I will offer later in this essay.

Other occasions also seemed like "church." For example, opening exercises of Sunday school for youth and adults were held in the sanctuary, including singing from the hymnals, announcements, prayer, and a special offering: an offering made by any person who had a birthday the prior week. While the groups sang "Happy Birthday," the birthday person(s) went to the front and put an offering in a receptacle shaped like a church. The expected gift was one cent for each year of one's age. The men of the church did not participate in these pre-Sunday school exercises. The men formed a large class downstairs, the Super Six Bible Class, a kind of church within the church, having its own music, offering, service projects, attendance check, prayers for the ill, and a Bible lecture very much like a sermon. No need to "stay for church."

I cannot identify all the reasons for my reluctance about "staying for church." Of course, the hour made it a long morning for a boy. And everything in worship seemed geared to adults, especially the sermons. Even so, I should have been more attracted to worship. The sanctuary was the most beautiful room I had experienced. The ceiling was high and lifted up; chandeliers and wall sconces lighted the large room. Pews were of dark wood, polished and beautiful. Leaded glass windows told stories of Jesus: Jesus holding a lamb, Jesus walking on the sea, Jesus knocking at a door, Jesus kneeling in prayer. Those windows carried me through many a lifeless service and dull sermon. They were formative for me. The mystery was too great for me. Bread from heaven? Cup of salvation? I think I was afraid something miraculous might happen. Even the offering, frequently treated as the collection of money, stirred in me a question: If we are giving to God, how does God get it? And the pulpit, on which lay open a gilt-edged Bible and from which came a word from God—well, let me return to the pulpit a bit later.

Maybe my hesitation, even resistance, to "staying for church" was due to an early and awkward reverence. I do not recall referring to the demand of the sanctuary on me as reverence. It felt like fear, born of the sense that God was in that room in a way different from God being in Sunday school class or youth meeting. There was no mystery in those places, but here there was *Mystery*. Mystery, almost palpable in its presence. In that room I was as aware of the supernatural as I was when Nicey Rounds, the midwife, warned me that demons could come out of the well at night if the cover was not on it. I wondered how worshipers could come into the sanctuary and visit with one another, laughing and talking before the service began. How could they? God was in this room; only silence was appropriate. So certain was I of this truth that slow and melancholy hymn singing, long and inaudible prayers at the table, dull and lifeless sermons—none of these singly or together could release me from the awe I felt in the sanctuary, whether in the company of the congregation or alone. And more and more I sought times there alone, believing as I did that if God ever spoke clearly to me about what to do with my life, it would be in that room God would speak. Now would be the appropriate time for me to say that as I matured in faith I came to understand that all places are the same, since God is everywhere. But I cannot say that. I know on one level that it is true; God does not need temples and sanctuaries. But I needed and still need places that are "The Places"; places where I can be refreshed by the presence of God. Immature and theologically inadequate? Probably, but "everywhere" seems a way of saying "nowhere." To this day, the one essential hour of a week is the hour in a place of worship. In my growing up, the sanctuary of Central Avenue Christian Church in Humboldt, Tennessee, was that place. The time came in those years when I no longer asked, "Do I have to stay for church?" I knew I had to stay, and not because Momma said so.

On occasion, out-of-town guests ask if I will show them the church of my upbringing. The tour always ends in the sanctuary. Anticipating their questions, I always point out five special places in the room. First, I walk to a particular pew, slightly beyond halfway to the rear and on the right side (as viewed from the front), and say "This is where I sat for worship with my mother and siblings." And your father? "Occasionally." "There were no cushions then, and the hymnals are different, but this is the place. There was no air conditioning and so in summer, hand fans from Hunt Funeral Home were in all the pew racks." Funeral home fans tended to lend sobriety to the service. The hymnals were objects of curiosity with words and music arranged for singing. Questions to Momma about the notes and music notations were answered, but not during the service. "Sh-h-h," she said. Then I walk my guests to the front of the sanctuary to the first pew in the center section. "This is where I stood in response to the minister's instruction and answered his question, 'Do you believe that Jesus is the Christ, the Son of the Living God, and do you accept him as your personal Savior?' I said 'Yes,' the minister blessed me, said a prayer for me, then the benediction. Afterwards, many of the members came to embrace me and offer encouraging words. It was for me a very emotional time."

The third "station" of the small tour is the baptistry. The baptistry in that church is not elevated, but rather on the level with the pews and almost in the right (viewed from the front) corner. When not is use, a maroon velvet curtain conceals it. "Here on a Sunday evening about three weeks following my confession I was baptized by our minister, Jack McCullough, in the name of the Father, the Son, and the Holy Spirit. Some of those present said I had 'joined the church.' It was more than that, but I did not know what. With my wet clothes under my arm, I walked home. I told my Mother I wanted to walk alone and I did. I prayed on the way and again in bed before going to sleep. I felt both uncertain and special, but also wondering if at school the next day any of my friends would have heard about my baptism. If not, should I tell them or was that special night between God and me?"

Next, I take my visitors again to the front of the sanctuary and in front of the Communion Table. The Table is at pew level and not elevated. In my tradition, the Table is not an altar, but more akin to a dining table around which a family gathers to share food and drink. "Here I was served my first Communion. I alone was served that Sunday evening, the congregation having shared in this service in morning worship. But the ritual was the same. An elder presided, reading one of the New Testament accounts of the Last Supper and reciting the words of institution. One offered a prayer of thanksgiving for the bread, the other for the cup. Then they served me quietly and reverently, returned the trays to the Table, and then joined the presiding elder in the Lord's Prayer, inviting me to join in the prayer. By this time the minister had come from the baptistry and, with a hand on my shoulder, dismissed the small assembly with a prayer of blessing and benediction. He and the three elders (all were male in those days) each shook my hand with a 'God bless you.' What an extraordinary day that was! All in one day, I had been buried with Jesus in baptism and had shared at his invitation at his Table. In all the years that followed I never experienced a day surpassing that one."

The fifth and final stop on the tour of the sanctuary is the pulpit. I always want my visitors to know where I, with much fear and trembling, first preached (if that is what it was). I recall to the visitors how I had as a boy so long admired and reverenced the pulpit: "On it rested the Bible, the Word of God. There was no place like it in all the world. And at the appointed time a man called of God to speak God's Word rose from a special chair, larger than other chairs, approached the pulpit, read from the Bible, prayed for guidance, and preached. He was not as other men, as was announced by his dress: striped trousers and morning coat. No other man in the sanctuary was attired as was the preacher. He was the preacher. It was the custom in those days, in that church, to address and to refer to the preacher as "Brother," but as a boy I thought "Brother" was not properly respectful. He was not my equal; he was my superior. In those days I did not know what else the minister did, but I did see him in the pulpit where he was God's preacher. I was in awe and accepted my not understanding what he talked about as further evidence of his special connection to God."

I cannot resist telling my visitors the keen disappointment I felt that day when, as an eighteen year old, I stood behind that pulpit. "I had never stood behind the pulpit; I had seen it only from the front. As I sat in the big chair (too big) waiting for the moment to stand and speak, I could see inside the pulpit. What a mess! A few broken hand fans, a clock, old worship bulletins, part of an angel's wing, golf tees, Christmas tree bulbs, a melted candle, and a glass of water with green scum on it. Obviously I preferred the view from the pew, but the choice no longer existed for me. The pulpit concealed as well as revealed. Many times I have wondered if I experienced a parable about preaching. Any tendency to be too enamored of the pulpit was dulled before I had preached my first sermon."

When I say that I had no role model among the preachers who stood in that pulpit, I mean no criticism or disrespect. Most of them possessed physical size and vocal volume that put them out of my reach at the outset. To attempt an imitation of them would have been foolish and carnivalesque. This is not to say they did not possess qualities worthy of an apprentice; they did. Frank Marler, the first minister I remember, was an example of a person whose conversion and call came as one dramatic move—as with Paul. He had been an FBI agent, a "G-man" as we called them. My friends and I were very interested in him, although I do not recall his speaking from the pulpit of his former life. So we had questions. Afraid to approach him individually, we stood around as a group after worship and, at breaks in his talking to parishioners, we moved in. "Did you carry a gun? Did you ever shoot anybody? Did you know Elliot Ness? Melvin Purvis? Were you ever shot? Do you still have your gun?" I don't think we ever asked him about Jesus, but he spoke to us about Jesus. He patiently tried to alter our interests and our questions and turned the conversations toward Jesus, the kind and loving and forgiving peacemaker. Perhaps he was partially successful. My mother did not favor his coming as our minister, but not because of his former life of violence. He was that ministerial candidate who, when introduced to the congregation, had had no hat and had worn a blazing red tie. As I mentioned earlier, for Momma he did not fit her image of a man of God. When he resigned years later, she confessed to him her early feelings, acknowledged he had proven her wrong, and wept at his departure.

The financial woes of the church in the 1930s and early 1940s translated into interim ministries and catching a few ministers on their way somewhere else. Even so, several made an impact on my life. I remember them in no particular chronological order. Jack McCullough, who baptized me, was finishing his seminary studies at Vanderbilt at the time and therefore was less available. He had been a professional football player, but he exercised admirable restraint and did not fill his sermons with stories of "my football days." He was big and strong but not intimidating; he was rather like a gentle bear.

John Porter paid the most attention to me, partially because he was my minister when I was really struggling about ministry as vocation. I was in high school and he discerned my wrestling. He was very approachable, informal, easy to talk with, and full of good humor. Momma said he was a good pastor and I'm sure she was right; he was to me. He was never intrusive, never hortatory, and never pressured me with emotional appeals. In fact, when I tried, in some desperation, to get him to make my decision for me, he deflected my effort. When I was sufficiently clear to say "yes" to God, he encouraged me to share it with the congregation. And it was he who urged me to preach even though I was as yet not even a college freshman. That was the frightening pulpit experience of an eighteen year old mentioned earlier. Following my brief disaster, he was the first to encourage me forward. John Porter was proud of his "Timothy," but I was never a notch on his belt.

When I was in grade school, Brother Frederick was briefly my minister. I know him by no other name, but I remember him clearly, and for three reasons. First, he came to our home, the little four-room house without electricity or indoor plumbing. He came on foot; whether he had a car I don't know. I was playing in the front yard. "Are your parents at home?" I ran inside yelling, "Momma, the preacher is here!" She came to the door, invited him in, and they talked a long time. About what? I don't know. Daddy and his drinking? Us kids and our need for clothes to wear to church? How Momma was managing? All or none of the above? No matter; the point is, the preacher of the church came to our home. For some reason, that was very important in my mind; maybe it gave our family status, or maybe something was wrong with our family. I chose the former interpretation of his visit and bragged of it to my friends. Soon thereafter some women from the church visited my mother and brought a box of children's clothes. A pair of shoes in the box fit me and I wore them to church.

Second, Brother Frederick returned some weeks later. I was in the side yard splitting wood for the kitchen stove. I heard him before I saw him. "Could you use some help?" I gladly relinquished the axe, and in a few minutes my pile of split wood had tripled. He wiped his brow, put on his coat, said, "Say hello to your folks for me," and walked away. Wow! He had not come to see my parents or my siblings; he had come to see *me*, no question.

He provided the third and final reason. I remember Brother Frederick at the door of the church following worship. Children grow accustomed to the generic greeting, "How are you, Sonny?" or, "How are you, Honey?" with the accompanying pat on the head. At least, it was my experience, even at church. That is, until Brother Frederick. He had hardly been at our church a month when it happened. Greeting departing worshipers at the door, he visited briefly with Momma and as I walked out behind her, he said, "How are you, Brenning? Are things going well at school?" He called me by my name. There is a world of difference between Brenning and Sonny; at least there was, and is, for me.

Let me tell briefly of another preacher who touched my life. This acknowledgment is not simply in retrospect; I was aware of his influences at the time. His name was Brother Foster; I am sorry I cannot identify him more precisely and I apologize to him. I could call the church and ask the secretary to pull his name from the file, but I am in the process of remembering and going to the records to supplement my memory feels unnecessary and unhelpful. It is enough to say that late in my grade school years there came to our church for a brief period a preacher I know as Brother Foster.

Brother Foster was older than our other preachers. Perhaps he interrupted his retirement to come to the aid of our church. He was neither short nor tall, neither heavy nor slight. He dressed so as to call no attention to himself: gray suits, white shirts, and ties in muted colors. He moved easily and with grace. His voice was strong enough to be heard, but not so strong that one *had* to hear him. He talked as though his listeners wanted to hear, as though they were informed and interested. He stood usually to the side of the pulpit, sometimes down in front of the pulpit. He talked, not at or to, but with the congregation. Nothing about him or his words was intimidating. He seemed to incarnate what might be called the modesty of God. He spoke without notes, but always with a small Bible in his hand to which he frequently referred, rereading key words and phrases. To a young boy he gave the impression that he knew personally the writers of the Bible, and maybe wrote some of it himself. I once asked Momma why he didn't raise his voice and sometimes yell as other preachers did. She said it was probably because he knew Jesus better than most and Jesus didn't yell and scream even when he preached outside on the street. I listened to Brother Foster with more care and delight than to any other preacher during my first eighteen years. I recall once saying to Momma that if ever I was a preacher, I probably would be like Brother Foster. But, of course, I said, I would *have to be,* since I was not big and strong and did not have much voice. She said that if I ever became a preacher God would provide a way for me to be heard. I recall saying no more. There was nothing more to be said at that time; I didn't have enough imagination to picture myself standing in a pulpit, or beside a pulpit, or on the floor beneath a pulpit.

11

Bethany Hills

In biographical and autobiographical writings there is a fairly common pattern: life as it was before a critical and defining experience or event; the critical and life-changing experience or event; life after that experience or event. The life being presented falls into two parts distinctly lying on either side of a clear and decisive moment. This has been the way of telling the stories of significant religious leaders: Paul, Augustine, Luther, Wesley, and countless others. But the pattern has been employed as well to describe significant lives in secular fields. "I was poor, confused, a failure, struggling aimlessly, trapped in bad circumstances and even worse decisions—and then it happened—and now fame, fortune, health, happiness, new friends and family, etc." No doubt, this is not only a literary pattern, a way of narrating, but a fairly accurate account of many lives.

Yet, as you have discerned from my recollections thus far, my life does not fit this pattern. I have struggled to identify "dots" in my life; that is, events or relationships that bore significantly on the direction of my life. In addition, I have struggled with "connecting these dots," that is, to understand these experiences as markers along a path to the pulpit. Two difficulties haunt the effort: one, realizing that I may have been significantly affected by a relationship or an event that my memory has not been able to retrieve. Two, recognizing that the appetite for meaning, for finding a path through the forest, for identifying the thread that makes a whole of parts, is so strong that connections and continuities are manufactured rather than discovered.

If I were pressed to offer a red-letter edition of myself, to underscore times or places or events which, as I now recall them, would come nearest to qualifying as that classical critical turning point, then I would say "Bethany Hills." Bethany Hills is a place, a camp and conference and retreat center owned and operated by the Christian Church (Disciples of Christ) in Tennessee. I remember it as being about twenty-five or thirty miles from Nashville, near Kingston Springs. Public transportation (bus) dropped me off at Kingston Springs, and someone from Bethany Hills, knowing my time of arrival, picked me up there. On my first trip there, the one picking me up was a man named Hamm, a retired Navy chaplain serving as one of the counselors. He was a hospitable man, preparing me for the place before we arrived. Upon arrival he pointed out the main features of the place: dining hall, boys dorm, girls dorm, lake, swimming pool, recreation area, office, and worship centers. Nothing fancy, he said, a bit rough and rustic, no air conditioning, he said, but you will come to love it, and at the end of the week you will hate to leave. He was right on all counts.

But Bethany Hills is more than a place; it is an experience. When I got off the bus I did not know what to expect; my sister had gone one year to church camp, but that was several years earlier and in a different location. "I had better have a good time," I told myself; after all, I was missing a week of work ($18.00) and had paid one-half the registration fee ($20.00, the church paid the other half). Such expense should guarantee wall-to-wall fun. Frieda, my sister, did not mention fun, but only said I would make new friends, a prospect not entirely inviting, given my hesitation in social situations. I went, I had fun, and I made new friends, some of which remain to this day.

However, "fun and friends" only touches the hem of the garment. Let me walk you through a day at Bethany Hills and perhaps you will sense the nature of the experience.

MORNING WATCH: Devotional time alone before breakfast. Beside the lake, under a tree, on a rock. Bible reading, prayer, notes on my thoughts, listening to the birds and to silence.

BREAKFAST: Simple food and not too much. Lots of noise, old friends renewing and remembering, meeting and exchanging names with the new; singing table-by-table, competing, several songs going at once—but all together on the Doxology.

CLASS: Four or five going at once: beside the lake, on a dorm porch, at an outdoor chapel, under a picnic shelter. Ministers, missionaries home on furlough, youth directors in local churches, these and others taught classes, all of which were oriented toward Christian commitment, whatever one's plans for college and vocation.

FREE TIME

CLASS: Rotate to another class. Informal but serious, open to all kinds of questions.

LUNCH: Simple food and not too much. Grace before the meal was sung, more noise and singing silly songs, loud talking, and mail call. (Surprising how many had letters, even on the first day). Calls for afternoon recreation: Archery, anyone? Softball, anyone? Horseshoes, anyone? Swimming, etc.

PREPARE FOR THE EVENING MEAL: And preparation time for those who signed up to help with evening worship.

EVENING MEAL: Simple food, plenty but not too much. Quieter conversation, singing but not silly, everyone is tired.

EVENING WORSHIP: Beside the lake. Getting dark. Birds and lightning bugs. Youth lead with singing, poems, Scripture readings, prayer. One of the counselors leads in a devotional reflection on the Scripture and on what a good day it has been.

POST-WORSHIP TIME: Conversations, pop, cookies, ice cream in the dining hall.

LIGHTS OUT: "Goodnight. See you in the morning."

Except, of course, for the few who do not give themselves to the program (homesick, amorous entanglements, general detachment from everything, parents divorcing, etc.) the rhythm of the days captures everyone. Minds wrap themselves around issues and events larger than self, and hearts open widely to each other and to God. Leaders do not impose a false solemnity on the week; the joy is unabated, although a heaviness breaks through now and them at mail call when a letter arrives from an older brother in uniform in Europe or the Pacific. World War II still rages. The contents of such letters resurface in the evening prayers. Toward the end of the week a number of the group begin to open up about considering ministry as a vocation. It seems natural, surrounded as we are by God and every bush on fire. The only unnatural feature of the week is the dress and speech of one boy who at sixteen behaves as a clerical caricature of himself. A teenager wearing black and sprinkling his speech with *King James* words—yuk! It is enough to lead some to repress or silence what otherwise might have been a healthy conversation about the call to ministry.

I certainly was not ready to talk to anyone about my being drawn toward the pulpit, not that first year at Bethany Hills. I do not say this in criticism of the teachers and counselors; they were comfortable to be with and good listeners. It was I who had nothing to say that could be taken as approaching a public or even a private declaration of a sense of call. I talked with only one person on this matter, and that was myself. My most serious conversation with myself about the direction of my life was in the form of a letter. Let me explain.

On Friday evening before our departure on Saturday morning, the worship service was especially moving. As we approached the worship center by the lake, we noticed the cross with a small open fire before it. Each was given a candle and during the singing of "Are Ye Able?" a flame from the open fire was given the first candle, from the first to the second, and on until everyone held a lighted candle. Wrapped in Scripture and prayer, instructions were given. We would leave the lake singing "We Are Climbing Jacob's Ladder" and, with the light of our candles, we were to make our way to the dormitories in total silence. In silence in the dorms we were to write letters addressed to ourselves. The letters would be mailed to us the next January. The silence was not to be broken until grace was said at breakfast. I wrote to myself my thoughts at the time, thoughts of God, church, family, friends—and ministry. I went to bed and, finally, to sleep.

The next January the letter came. It surprised me; after all, it had been written six months earlier. I waited for a time and place of privacy to open the letter. I wanted the reading to match the writing as much as possible. The letter revived in me that closing worship and I worshiped again. In the letter I made an "almost promise" to God. By "almost" I refer to the contingency: if God would give me some sign, some ground for certainty of call, I would, following graduation from high school, begin preparation for Christian ministry. I recall no wish for an extraordinary shout of divine call; a good clear whisper would suffice. My letter closed with a promise to listen carefully for that whisper.

And I did listen, from January to June, at which time I returned to youth conference at Bethany Hills. In many ways the second year was better than the first: I knew the place, the schedule, and most of the attendees, many of whom had become friends the previous year. In fact, I had seen some of them at a mid-winter CYF (Christian Youth Fellowship) conference held in Nashville. I could name for you a dozen or so who remain good friends more than six decades later.

The principal difference from the first year was in me. I was a year older and had January till June to think further about my letter to myself. At the closing worship service I again wrote the letter but this time I removed the contingency; the request for a clear sign of God's call was dropped. The reasons were two: one, my pastor had preached a strong sermon on "you shall not put God to the test"; and two, I was more certain of the call to ministry. However, during the next year that certainty came under multiple attacks, as I will explain later. Perhaps certainty was an idol erected in my mind, and in some sense a contradiction rather than a confirmation of faith.

During my second year at Bethany Hills I was more ready to talk about my life and possible vocational future. I had become more socialized at home through school and church functions, but it was at church camp that I was more open to deal with the question, "What are you going to do after high school?" My general answer was, "Go to college," but to a few I was ready to talk of ministry. It helped that I was not alone in the interest; probably as many as three dozen of the conferees were at my point vocationally—some more, some less clear in their direction.

Now that I think back on that time in my life, the ending of World War II removed a complicating variable from my decision about ministry. Had the war continued another year I would have had to choose between Momma's pacifism and Daddy's military patriotism. In some ways I wanted to have to make that decision: I was not old enough for the draft. As irrational as it seems, I felt a bit guilty for being younger than Walter and Alvin. When scarce and sparse news came from Walter in the jungles of the Philippines or from Alvin aboard a Landing Ship Vehicle off the coast of Japan, what was I doing to deserve being their brother? Getting ready for a football game, or a date, or just going to hang out at the drugstore with my friends? Big deal! When those letters came from life-and-death zones of the Pacific, I sat between my mother's tears and my father's pride, feeling very insignificant. Neither my parents nor my older brothers made me feel that way; the feeling was imbedded in the situation. Had the war lasted another year and I stood before the draft board in the county courthouse in Trenton to declare my decision for Christian ministry, that act could easily have been branded "draft dodging." Reading my own heart was difficult enough, so how could I read the mind of the public? I couldn't, but I did.

But now the war was over; Walter was home and resuming his education, Alvin was home and enjoying it before turning the next corner of his life, and I was at Bethany Hills talking about becoming a minister, set free no less than they by the ending of the war. You can imagine how emotional was my prayer of thanksgiving for the war's end that night by the lake when we sang "Are Ye Able?" by candlelight. God has been especially good to me, I thought in the silence of the walk to the dorm where I again wrote a letter to myself. I almost addressed the letter "Dear God," rather than "Dear Brenning."

My most significant, and frequent, conversation partners during that second year at Bethany Hills were ministers. Older ministers. In reflection from this distance, I am struck by the presence, the influential presence, of senior ministers at gatherings of teenagers. Apparently I am reporting on a time before the churches decided to turn their young people over to young ministers, some of them but a few years older than their charges. Perhaps the generation gap needed to be collapsed. This is not the time or place to weigh the merits of that conclusion. Lacking the presence of youth ministers or young ministers, my conference experience provided no test case showing that, given a choice, young people will gravitate toward a younger rather than an older minister. I can only report that the ministers available to us were older and I can report that gravitate toward them we did. In my experience they were present, available, nonintrusive, good listeners, of good humor, and genuinely interested in my life and my vocation. In all my conversations with them, the subject was the same: call to ministry. Three of them stand out in my memory as being especially wise, sympathetic, and helpful. Each of them was appropriately addressed as Doctor, each having received the honorary Doctor of Divinity degree.

Dr. T. O. Slaughter was pastor of Decatur Christian Church in Memphis, and he provided guidance at the Bethany Hills camp. During his long ministry, a score or more of young people from his congregation entered the ministry. At camp, they spoke of him with respect and with affection. I noticed that he also was in conversation with youth who were not of his flock. His voice was gentle and inviting. He knew me before I knew him, and welcomed me into small informal circles as well as on occasions when I sought him out alone. He talked of the joys and burdens of ministry, of the struggle to be certain of God's call. He was steeped in Scripture, from which he drew example after example of persons being called of God for special tasks. "God calls in different ways," he said, "tempering the wind to the shorn lamb." Be patient and prayerful. "One way you will know God's call," he said, "is to feel you *have* to be a minister, to be unable to imagine yourself doing anything else." He never pressed me for an answer to "Have you decided yet?" He seemed comfortable leaving the matter between God and me. When I was sure, I wanted him to know; and on a trip to Memphis for a West Tennessee CYF Retreat I told him. He was pleased and, I think, not surprised.

Dr. Frank Drowota was pastor of the newly formed Woodmont Christian Church in Nashville. He had come to Nashville from Kentucky, but he was a native of England. His place of origin was evident in his speech, only partially concealed in an unusual raspiness. In our conversations, unlike Dr. Slaughter who focused on Scripture, Dr. Drowota had me recalling family and school and church relationships. God often calls to ministry indirectly through other people. He spoke of his own life, perhaps as a way to get me to open up about mine. In no way did he offer his own experiences as normative, but he did help me to understand that God is not coercive, but sometimes is modest, making claims on us in small but important ways. The voice of a parent or teacher or friend may be the vehicle for God's voice. "Whoever has ears to hear," he said to me quite often. As with Dr. Slaughter, I detected in him no sarcasm or cynicism about the ministry.

And I certainly did not hear it in Dr. Roger Nooe. Dr. Nooe was pastor of Vine Street Christian Church in Nashville. I was somewhat in awe of him, having heard of his leadership in the denomination and in the city of Nashville. His reputation as a great preacher was confirmed to me later on the occasions when I heard him speak. But nothing of his greatness prompted an aloofness or an inaccessibility at Bethany Hills. He was full of good humor and poetic in expression. However, my two most helpful encounters with him were not at Bethany Hills. One was in Nashville at Vine Street on the Saturday afternoon following the Saturday morning closing of our camp week. Transportation arrangements for several of us from West Tennessee called for going into Nashville, where we were to be picked up. We sat in the sanctuary of Vine Street Church, waiting. During our wait, Dr. Nooe came out of his study, welcomed us, and for almost an hour held us spellbound with stories from his life, especially his early years. There he was, *the* Dr. Nooe, giving himself to six or seven camp-tired teenagers. Apparently that was where he wanted to be and that was what he wanted to do.

My second significant encounter was about a year later in a small restaurant near Dickson, Tennessee, about forty miles west of Nashville. He was on his way home from Memphis, and I was on my way home from Nashville. He was already seated and had ordered when I entered. I did not see him. But he saw me, came over, called me by name, introduced himself, as though I would not remember him, and asked if we might eat together. I was in awe, but soon we were remembering Bethany Hills, people and events. He rose to leave first, and as he left, he came back to the table to say, "If I were God, I would call you into the ministry without a moment's hesitation." My right hand may forget its cunning, my tongue may cleave to the roof of my mouth, but I will never forget his words nor will my tongue tire of repeating them.

12

The Summer of '46

Following high school graduation in May 1946, my life began to move according to my plan. I was going into Christian ministry. I had said so to God, to my friends and counselors at Bethany Hills, to my family, to my hometown friends, and to my home church. Such notifications were important, said my pastor, Brother John Porter, not only because all these people would be happy about my decision, but their knowing would help seal the decision in case I had days when I got cold feet. I would not get cold feet, I told him; my direction was clear.

What was not clear was choice of a college. Here I had little help. Classmates who were going to college enrolled where parents had gone or where scholarships were offered. I had, because of my grades, been contacted by several schools, including the one I most favored, the University of Missouri School of Journalism. But these offers preceded my decision for ministry and in my mind, a degree from one of these colleges or universities would only be a detour, a delay of four years. No one told me that a degree in journalism or history or literature or psychology would be excellent preparation for seminary. Once I declared for ministry the high school teacher who functioned as vocational counselor fell silent. She had no clue about preparation for the ministerial life. She simply said I would need to attend a seminary and referred me to my pastor.

Two considerations were clear to me: I wanted to move directly toward preparation for ministry. Brother Porter said I could not go directly to a seminary; I had first to get a college degree. That sounded like a delay, but if that was the norm, fine. So where do I go to college? The "where" would have to be inexpensive: I had tossed the offers of scholarships, my family had no money, and I had no money. I felt alone in a strange land. My friends who headed for Lambuth or Union or Vanderbilt or the University of Tennessee seemed to be on a clear, well-traveled road. Not I. It was as though I were the first person in history to begin academic preparation for ministry. And I was running late; it is not a long way from May to September.

Brother Porter suggested I contact two colleges: Berea College in Berea, Kentucky, and Johnson Bible College, Kimberlin Heights, Tennessee, near Knoxville. Both schools, he said, opened their doors to the poor by providing opportunities for students to work their way through. Berea, in fact, required all students to work: on the grounds, in food service, in the bookstore, in janitorial service, etc. At Johnson, working on campus was not required but practically everyone did. It was a farm school with crops, chickens, turkeys, and a dairy herd. There was plenty of work; one could enroll without a dime and work off all costs: room, board, tuition, and books. Both schools responded to my inquiries and seemed pleased to have me. Berea offered more liberal arts courses while Johnson had a noticeably Bible-centered curriculum. Where to go, now that the financial question was not a hurdle?

Brother Porter voted for Johnson. While he had good things to say about Berea (he had not attended either school), he thought Johnson would give me a strong foundation for seminary later. That was persuasive; I certainly did not want to walk into a seminary and be the only one who knew nothing of Bible, church history, or theology. And, I said to myself, it is in Tennessee. At the time I had never been out of the state and Kentucky seemed much farther from home. Not important now; very important then. I filled out an application and was accepted. In the Fall of 1946 I would be attending Johnson Bible College.

Already I had a job for the summer in my hometown. B.C. Jarrell and Co. manufactured wooden containers for shipping fruits and vegetables. Late spring and summer was the peak time for an agricultural economy and there were short-term jobs a plenty, in field and factory. My job at B.C. Jarrell was making small wooden boxes or lugs for packing and shipping tomatoes. The pre-cut pieces came along on a belt, the pieces were assembled on a small table beside the belt, all held in place with twenty-four nails. The work was competitive in that there were several workers at tables alongside the belt. After a few days of splinters, bent nails, and very sore muscles, I found my rhythmic movement and the work became routine and, most importantly, lucrative. We were paid "by the piece" and I turned out my share of pieces. My first check was for $37.00, $30.00 of which began a bank account. At that rate, after ten weeks I would have $300.00 for school shirts, sweaters, trousers, and a bus ticket. But I overestimated: the foreman told me it was a union factory and I would have to pay union dues. The third week the foreman said we were striking because of poor working conditions. The strike lasted fifteen days. I was not unsympathetic with the union but I needed money, and fast. The financial blow was softened somewhat by an older cousin who twice slipped a twenty-dollar bill into my hand after Sunday worship.

Another fifteen dollars came my way, but it was the hardest earned fifteen dollars in my life. When the strike interrupted cash flow, Brother Porter came by the house with an offer. He was to preach every night that next week in a church up the road, maybe fifty miles, in the town of Gleason. He had told the folk there about me and they accepted his suggestion that I preach one night and for it they would give me fifteen dollars.

"But I have never preached!"

"They know that."

"But I don't have a sermon!"

"You have a week to prepare one."

"But how do I do that?"

"We learn by doing."

"I have no way to get to Gleason!"

"I'll take you and pay for your supper; that way, the fifteen dollars will be clear profit."

"I'll bet no one will show up to hear a scared and stupid teenager!"

"No, that night we will probably have our best crowd."

"Yeah, curious to see how I would make a fool of myself." But how could I say no? Had I not publicly declared for Christian ministry?

The next week was misery upon misery. What would I say? After several dead ends, I decided to talk about the wise men coming to worship Jesus. My plan was to read the text, have a prayer, paraphrase what I had read, and then urge everyone to worship and follow Jesus. I calculated it would take twelve minutes. I was wrong; I was through in five, including two interruptions. No one had warned me that in regular attendance was a man mentally and emotionally challenged. He often interrupted preachers. Interruption number one: "You said three wise men; how do you know there were three?" "I don't know." Interruption number two: "Who was the meanest woman in the Bible?" Again, "I don't know." My life was over. I had flunked ministry, Bible, and preaching. I could not be consoled. On the way home, Brother Porter's words fell on deaf ears. There would be no time to redeem myself; there would be no second chance. In one night I managed to begin and to end my career in the pulpit.

As I remember that night after all these years, I still feel the dark and dismal heaviness of it. And along with that memory comes the recollection of the downward spiral of my spirit during which I sought reasons for disqualifying myself, for trashing my plans, for taking my night of failure as a sign from God that I was not called. I had been deluding myself. I did not begin my new negativity by making a 180° turnabout, by converting my earlier "Yes" into a "No." I began with the idea of postponement. I could wait a year, get a job, save money, seriously study the Bible, prepare a better sermon, practice it, and who knows, maybe get a chance to redeem myself at Gleason. I did not, at the time, see how central was my pride, my ego, in this new line of reasoning. Neither did I admit to myself an additional motivation: I had recently begun dating Nettie Lee Dungan. I felt strongly that the relationship had a future (we have now been married fifty-eight years), a future I could nourish by sticking around another year, but not by going away to college.

While I entertained the postponement reasoning and while unemployed due to the strike, I said "Yes" to an invitation to return to Bethany Hills, this time as a worker, as a counselor intern, replacing someone who had to drop out. My "Yes" to the invitation was with enthusiasm: *Good, get out of town, heal from the Gleason tragedy, get some positive reinforcement, and reexamine your "Yes" to God in the very place so influential in your having said "Yes" in the first place.* It was possible, I thought, for my "Yes," slowly becoming a "No," to become a "Yes" again.

Boy, was I wrong! The very place through which God had enthralled me into ministry now turned on me. The trees, the lake, the hills, the vesper spot, the skits, the songs, the candles—now I saw them for what they were: together one huge, beautiful, irresistible trap to ensnare romantic and idealistic teenagers. With one sweet voice they said, "God wants you to be a preacher." Who could say "No"? I recalled the nights following the lakeside consecration services when I lay on my cot in silence, dreamily fantasizing about what it meant to give my life to God. How do you give your life to God? A child darts in front of a speeding car; you save a life but lose your own. A swimmer cramps up in the ocean surf; you jump in and save a life but lose your own. You are a missionary in some inhospitable country. You are blindfolded, placed against a wall as the firing squad moves into place. Ready! Aim! Fire! Women weep, the flag is at half-mast, a monument is erected, and tourists pause for photos beside the martyr's grave. What moving images, inspiring and idealistic! And of no more reality than a bubble; eye-catching for a moment, then "pop!" and then gone. This was Bethany Hills, wrapped in beauty and vision, but not real. I was called to ministry in an unreal world, I told myself, and I said it with the voice of one who took his call to the real world and was silenced by a disoriented stranger in Gleason. The candle lit by the lake at Bethany quickly melted in the heat of a world that said, "This is the way it really is. Do you have any more sermons, Preacher?"

I returned to reality, to driving nails, to foul-mouthed fellow workers, to a town full of racial and economic prejudices, to indifferent churches, to the few with too much, to the many with too little, to summer revivals threatening with hell and teasing with heaven. Floyd, standing next to me beside the belt bringing the makings of a tomato lug, stopped his hammer.

"Your name Brenning?"

"Yes."

"Are you the one they say is making a preacher?"

"Yes."

"The hell you say. Have you been *called* to preach?"

After a pause, I said, "Yes."

What just happened? At a time when I had been trying to say "No" to God, I said "Yes" to Floyd. Had Floyd just called me into the ministry? Floyd was probably fifty years old, had a wife and four children, and needed every dollar he could make at the seasonal and part-time jobs he could find. He had almost no education, had been nowhere, was going nowhere, and talked incessantly about that really good-paying job he was going to get, but he was going nowhere to get it. He felt superior to Blacks, Mexicans, Germans, Japanese, and women who had office jobs. The only light on his horizon was a cold beer. Who was he to engage me in conversation about the ministry?

The "Yes" I said to Floyd came as a revelation: God sometimes calls through one's realization of the needs of people among whom one lives. Floyd and the hundreds like him in my little town were not the "reality" to discourage me from ministry, but rather the reality shouting out the need for ministry. Maybe Bethany Hills did its work to make me more sensitive to human needs, more open in mind and heart and hand to persons who otherwise would be invisible and silent. I recalled the answer a missionary home on furlough gave to my question, "Why did you go to the Congo as a missionary?" "Somebody had to go." At the time the answer seemed uninspired and disappointing. I expected a moving testimony of God at work in his life; what I got was a straightforward, "The need was there and somebody had to meet it." Maybe this was the bare bones, no fanfare call I needed to hear: if one is made alive and aware of human need then that in itself is the call. Look out on the world rather than probing within trying to locate the "gifts and graces" for ministry. Years later I was to call such an experience hearing "the groan of God," a phrase borrowed from the apostle Paul. My world suddenly grew larger and deeper; there was room for both Bethany Hills and Gleason, and much more.

I was back on track; I drove nails and saved money. But I also enjoyed lunch break with Floyd, Howard, Butch, and Bobby. Over sandwiches we shared our lives. I learned children's names and met wives on Friday afternoons when the factory whistle announced the weekend. I took as compliments the jokes and the advice given, most of it having to do with my short stature and soft voice. They did not see why I had to go to school if I had been called, but they wished me well. In early August I was to preach at the regular Sunday worship service. I invited all my friends at work. Their vague responses said they probably would not be there. They weren't; nothing personal, just a matter of their understanding of churches, especially brick churches on nice street corners in town. Parting handshakes were genuine.

Brother Porter thought it would be appropriate for me to preach to our congregation before I left for school. It would help the church measure how much I had improved when I next preached after some schooling. I accepted and immediately became nervous. I had two weeks to prepare. Brother Porter brought to my home a little book of "sermon starters." "I've preached the fire out of that book," he explained. I took it but found it useless, even in my desperation. I settled on John 10 as my text and "The Good Shepherd" as my topic. I remember having two parts to the sermon: Jesus ministers to us as a Good Shepherd, and as a Good Shepherd he shows us how we should help each other. I had no resources for preparation. In the church office was a small library of "quaint and curious" volumes, among which I found a Bible dictionary, a one-volume commentary on the New Testament, and a concordance. I was somewhat supported by my "research," but intimidated by the concordance. There were so many uses of the word *shepherd* in the Bible I was almost scared away from my subject. I closed my eyes to everything but John 10. I took into the pulpit about eight handwritten pages of script. I calculated that would last sixteen minutes; I was through in ten.

In the pulpit I was tense and nervous. Family and relatives were there; high school friends were there; Nettie Lee was there. The increased attendance was encouraging but added to my nervousness. I wondered if the inquisitor from Gleason was there. Surely not. I half-read, half-recited my script. Afterward Brother Porter said I did well, as did Nettie Lee and a number of others. High school friends offered more roast than toast, but all in good-humored encouragement.

On Sunday afternoon I spent some time alone in self-assessment. Now, after more than sixty years, I remember some of my reflections, probably because they still occupy my mind when I debrief myself after preaching. Let me mention four lines of thought.

One, I belonged in the pulpit. Of all the tasks of ministry, preaching should be my focus. There are many important and essential ministries without a pulpit, all of them of God, but I must have a pulpit. This is not a commentary on my weaknesses, already in evidence that August, 1946 Sunday, and therefore, the area to which I must give major attention. Nor is it a commentary on my strengths, present in embryo that Sunday. Neither was in my mind. All I can say is that preaching "fit"; I should be in the pulpit. Call? I don't know. Ego? I don't know.

Two, the nervousness I felt was a different kind of nervousness. I had quite recently given the valedictory speech at high school graduation and I was nervous, but this was different. This was tension, the way one's body registers the importance of what one is doing. The constellation of elements: prayers, Scripture, the Eucharist, congregational singing, the presence of God, and the expectation conspired to give the occasion almost frightening significance. What if God used the sermon to effect a change in or among persons in attendance? Who wants to be an accessory to life-altering? This describes the "stage fright" I had, and still have.

Three, standing at the door and greeting worshipers as they leave is not for me. Several factors are involved. The worshipers are trapped; what is to be said, if anything? Emotionally I am still in the pulpit; friendly visits at the door come too soon. A chat with the preacher is a quick and easy way to remove the provocation of the sermon; on to the cafeteria. Besides, liking or not liking the sermon is hardly a desired conclusion to preaching the Gospel. However, being an unfriendly pastor is hardly the answer. Someone present really needs to speak with the preacher. Have a designated place after worship where such conversation can take place.

Finally, I experienced greater pleasure (pleasure is not always inappropriate) in the preparation of the sermon than its delivery. Thin and inadequate as it was, the study time was sacred time, time of being open, vulnerable, and receptive to the presence of God. Delivery can be such, as well, but during delivery there are so many variables that the preacher has to work very hard to keep focus. And, of course, my own early life was and is still with me: a large interior world, comfortable being alone, undersocialization. I was later to hear from a rabbi, "An hour at study is in the sight of the Holy One, blessed be He, as an hour of prayer."

The summer of 1946 moved swiftly to its close. More time with Nettie Lee, gathering a few clothes (I would need only enough for one week, the school said; the students did their laundry every Saturday or Monday), getting a complete Bible (Miss Emma Sloan's gift had only been a New Testament with Psalms), visits with friend, talks with Momma, and asking God if there were any last-minute instructions—this was it. In these undramatic ways I prepared to leave.

Early morning is not a good time to leave, but neither is afternoon or evening. Purchasing the bus ticket was almost final. Stepping onto the Greyhound bus was final—almost, but not quite: the bus stopped frequently and I could have gotten off anytime. Getting off the bus in Knoxville eight hours later, that seemed final, except there was yet thirteen miles on a local bus out to Kimberlin Heights. The walk from the drop off at Jigg's Store seemed like the last mile, but I could still change my mind. Down the road, past the barn, on a hill overlooking the French Broad River, sat Johnson Bible College. I approached what was obviously the Main Building. Over the entrance were the words:

Open day and night to the poor young man who desires above every other desire to preach the Gospel of Christ.

I entered, and that was final.

"My name is Brenning Craddock." So I responded to the woman helping to herd college freshman through orientation. "Your name?" she asked, not even looking up, her voice quite indifferent. "Brenning Craddock," I repeated. "Beg pardon?" "Brenning Craddock." "I'm sorry?" "Brenning Craddock." "You'll have to spell it." "F-R-E-D." She felt my disgust and said, "Next; your name please." Thus began the life of Fred Craddock.

13

Reflections on These Reflections

I actually thought at the outset that, in the process of my memory moving among the dots (events, places, persons), I would be able to identify "The Dot," the source of certainty to use in answering the high school and college question, "When did you know for sure that God had called you to preach?" Well, as you know, I didn't find it, or at least I didn't identify it. Not that I think the certainty-producing moment is absolutely essential. A call is of a piece with one's entire life of faith; it may be made up of a constellation of small things: a stanza of a hymn, a child's prayer, a friend's presence, a verse of Scripture, a greeting card, an evening walk, or an encounter with a stranger. A recital of modest events may not add up to a testimony satisfactory to everyone, but I am sustained by it. In fact, I believe one could preach for a lifetime and yet not satisfy one's own or another's desire for certainty. But does an element of uncertainty invalidate one's acts of ministry: preaching, praying, presiding, pastoring, baptizing? Not at all. The church has agreed with Augustine over Donatus: the efficacy of God's Word is not dependent on the faith of the one who is its messenger.

Having said this rather assuredly, I must confess that at times I could have earnestly prayed John Donne's prayer:

Batter my heart, three-personed God; for you
As yet but knock, breathe, shine, and seek to mend.

* * * * * * *

It seems to me now that my search for clarity about "call," while necessarily personal, was unnecessarily private. I had conversation partners, to be sure, but I opened up to them only after I had enough sense of direction to remain in at least partial control of the conversation. For example, I *announced* my intention to be a minister to various groups: family, friends, and congregation, but how many of them were partners in the process of discernment? Very, very few. As a result, no one grew by making the trip with me, and I grew the less without them. I did not allow God to use the persons around me; I did not allow the church to be the church. I regret that. I know what I was thinking: *This is between God and me, one on one, and all others are nonparticipants.* As you probably noticed, I let a select few into the circle, but on my timing, and they were persons who would say what I wanted to hear. But in my hungering for a defining experience of God as the one who calls, I sincerely thought of most others as distractions. In other words, stay off the phone, I'm expecting a call!

* * * * * * *

I am embarrassed that I came rather late (if age eighteen is late) to the realization that God also calls by pointing to needs and opening one's eyes to see them. For example, African Americans were friends, neighbors, and playmates, but schools and churches were totally segregated, and I heard no adult voices raised against the system. I never heard a sermon that even alluded to the situation. That was the way our world was. I was not a child prophet, but I did ask why my friend J.W. and I could not go to school together. Working and observing and listening at B.C. Jarrell's made me aware of, even afraid of, the economic and racial prejudices built into our culture. As early as 1946 there were incidents almost incendiary. Slowly, but only slowly, did I begin to see social components of preaching the Gospel.

* * * * * * * *

I think I have used only once the generally familiar phrase "gifts and graces for ministry." The reasons for such limited use are two: one, it was not at that time a phrase current in the circles in which I lived and thought. Two, I have not been comfortable asking, in whatever phrasing, "Do I have the gifts and graces for ministry?" Perhaps it is a question not for me but for persons examining me prior to ordination. But who can say for sure? By "gifts and graces," do we mean that one is friendly, extroverted, articulate, and of good reputation? Perhaps; those are qualities admirable and to be desired. But a person reticent and undersocialized may in time grow into a life fitted beautifully for Christian service. Sometimes, persons rise to the top who lack all those immediate gifts that tend to detain you at the bottom. And it is not uncommon for such gifts not even to appear until a crisis or a strong need sounds reveille and every quality of mind, body, and soul bends to the task.

* * * * * * * *

It is possible to get bogged down in excessive inwardness. We want to experience feelings appropriate to a task; that is, we want actions to be from the heart, we want actions to be confirmed by the pulse. Of course we do, but must the appropriate feeling *precede* the action? Must we wait until heart and mind fully agree before we lend voice and hand to an endeavor? It is possible that the feeling we desire will follow rather than precede the action. One may feel fear and run, it is true, but it is also true that one can run and by running generate fear. Tinkering with right feelings can be for ministry a delay tactic in the face of problems complex and pressing for response. Perhaps someone should have said to me, "You may decide for ministry by only 51 percent, but once you do, give it 100 percent and very likely someone will approach you to ask, 'You seem so certain; when and where did it come to you?'"

* * * * * * * *

I have not in these reflections isolated "will" as a factor in a call to preach, and probably it is too late to bring it up now. Will has been implied, of course, in the idea of deciding "Yes" or "No." As much as one wants to honor divine initiative, as much as one wants to think of one's life as part of a metanarrative, transcending all endeavors that are launched with "I decided to—," the fact is, I decided to be a preacher. I cannot divide the work so simply as to say "God called" and "I decided," as though it were a drama in two acts. When I was thinking this way, I stalled out, waiting. My present view is that the call is in the response, in the decision. Perhaps I came to this conclusion under the influence of Jesus as presented in the gospel of John: "Anyone who resolves to do the will of God will know whether the teaching is from God or whether I am speaking on my own" (7:17, NRSV). Willing to do precedes rather than follows knowing. Or maybe this sequence came as a partial recollection of the ending of Albert Schweitzer's *Quest for the Historical Jesus*: Jesus commands, we obey, and in the process of doing his work we come to know who he is. At this moment comes an even more remote recollection from Franz Werfel's *The Song of Bernadette*. He concludes his preface to the story of this girl's extraordinary experience of God with the reminder that to the one who wills to believe, final proof is not necessary; to the one who will not believe, final proof is never enough.

Yes, I decided to be a preacher, and the decision preceded final proof. The truth is, there was no final proof. One can toss the fleece, as did Gideon (Judg. 6:36–40), not once, not twice, not a thousand times, and have the undeniable proof. Sooner or later one has to decide, unless, of course, one wishes to make a career of fleece tossing. But then that, too, is a decision.

* * * * * * * *

And, there is always room to decide. In retrospect, I can see that at times I was asking others to make my decision: my mother, my pastor, my counselors at youth camp. But, bless them, they all turned the decision back to me. And they understood that my "Yes" would not hold up unless a reasonable "No" was available. I say a reasonable "No," not a weak, crippled, thoughtless, afraid, and fruitless "No," as though it was the pulpit or the pits. Life is no cartoon; a "No" could have taken me to pleasant and prosperous and respected places. Let's keep the competition fair.

In 1969, on a trip to Israel with my family, it seemed wise, given the circumstances, to secure the services of someone who not only had a vehicle but who knew where, and where not, to go. His name was Jonas, a veteran of the Israeli army. We were in Bethlehem when Jonas began to explain how a few uneducated shepherds could come up with their "night stories," not with malicious intent, Jonas explained. It is commonly known, he said, that the illiterate often entertain superstitions, giving them some relief from lives empty of meaning. Jonas was serious, thoughtful, and reasonable. When he finished, I thanked him for his interpretation but reminded him that as Christians we understood the Bethlehem story differently. He welcomed my alternative with this explanation: "Unless something can be explained at least two different ways, then God had nothing to do with it." In other words, in God's world, there is room to believe and not believe.

As for me, I believe God called me to preach; or, to put it another way, I decided to be a preacher. Or, as Paul might put it, "I seek to lay hold of him who has already laid hold of me."

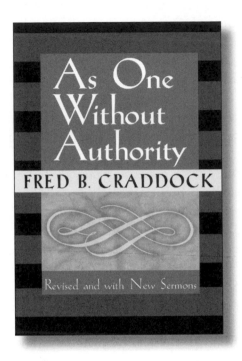

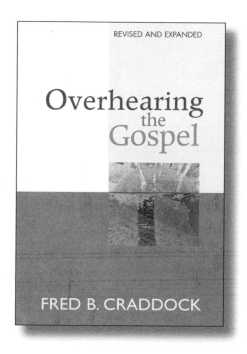

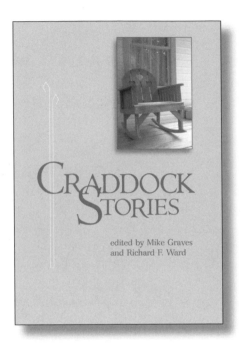